Entering Eternity Today

God's Kingdom Revealed On Earth

By
Tim Sweetman

Since we are receiving a kingdom that is unshakable, let us be thankful and please God by worshipping him with holy fear and awe.
Hebrews 12:28.

Acknowledgements

Thank you to the Spirit of God for continuing to open up the scriptures in these times.

Thank you to John, my brother, for some of the teaching that is the backbone for the contents of this book.

Thank you to my friends, Mark and Chris, for prompting me to write on this subject, to Pete and my children for the additional questions and for those of you who have been the reason for much of the research involved in establishing some truth amongst so much misunderstanding.

Preface:

I have spent many years receiving revelation, unearthing, researching and writing with regards to misunderstandings of scripture that are commonly taught and accepted amongst church circles.

These are widespread and general, which lead to a dysfunctioning of God's people.

We fall short of our purpose and destiny because we do not understand the reason Jesus came, what He achieved or what our purpose within that is.

The Lord will not allow the harvest that is to come until we understand and take hold of His good news.

The enemy has spread a gospel that is misleading, untrue and counter productive; it is a gospel that ensures that his kingdom will not be overthrown.

Many well known and famed ministers of religion preach this false gospel and millions of Jesus' followers are led astray.

I have been overwhelmed recently when discovering just how deep and blatant the lies that the enemy has spread amongst us are, and how many of us are deceived by them.

If we are to gain any ground there is a necessity to rediscover what Jesus and His followers taught and to follow where that truth might lead us.

Until we do, the enemy will continue to have his way.

The reader will find some repetition within these pages, albeit coming from alternative points of perspective.

The repetition is intentional.

Jesus very often repeated His teaching in various ways, through symbolism, parables, life pictures and miracles in order to emphasise what He was saying.

Paul and other writers of scripture also repeat their teaching, using different words in order to convey their meaning better.

We are very forgetful humans and being reminded of a phrase or lesson occasionally can sometimes be necessary.

I would appreciate any queries and feedback on the contents of this book.

A new revelation is often received with some surprise if it contradicts what we have believed previously and so please take some time to consider both the scriptures and what God's Spirit is saying to you personally.

Introduction:

Over a period of some two thousand years the church has been soaked; immersed, in a counterfeit religion.

One of the aspects of this counterfeit religion is the doctrine that teaches we must wait until we die before we will inhabit Heaven.

Another is that Jesus will, one day return to take His children away to live with Him in Heaven - the doctrine of the rapture.

There are, sadly, many other false teachings.

We have been taught that Heaven awaits us somewhere and perhaps, one day, Jesus will return to take us there.

In the reading of this book we will discover that there are no scriptures to support these doctrines.

On the contrary, Jesus and His followers taught a very different gospel.

The good news that Jesus brought is a very different gospel to the one that is taught by religious preachers, from pulpits, day after day.

We will uncover a new way of living with Jesus today and into eternity, when we look at the truth that Jesus taught, and the enemy will not like what we discover.

When we encounter and live in the true gospel the enemy will flee, and Jesus will set loose a harvest of souls that we can only imagine.

Isaiah's Good News of God's kingdom.

The Spirit of the Sovereign Lord is upon me, for the Lord has anointed me to bring good news to the poor.

He has sent me to comfort the brokenhearted and to proclaim that captives will be released and prisoners will be freed.

He has sent me to tell those who mourn that the time of the Lord's favor has come, and with it, the day of God's anger against their enemies.

To all who mourn in Israel, he will give a crown of beauty for ashes, a joyous blessing instead of mourning, festive praise instead of despair.

In their righteousness, they will be like great oaks that the Lord has planted for his own glory.

They will rebuild the ancient ruins, repairing cities destroyed long ago.

They will revive them, though they have been deserted for many generations.

Foreigners will be your servants.

They will feed your flocks and plough your fields and tend your vineyards.

You will be called priests of the Lord, ministers of our God.

You will feed on the treasures of the nations and boast in their riches.

Instead of shame and dishonour, you will enjoy a double share of honour.

You will possess a double portion of prosperity in your land, and everlasting joy will be yours. "For I, the Lord, love justice.

I hate robbery and wrongdoing.

I will faithfully reward my people for their suffering and make an everlasting covenant with them.

Their descendants will be recognized and honoured among the nations.

Everyone will realise that they are a people the Lord has blessed."

I am overwhelmed with joy in the Lord my God!

For he has dressed me with the clothing of salvation and draped me in a robe of righteousness.

I am like a bridegroom dressed for his wedding or a bride with her jewels.

The Sovereign Lord will show his justice to the nations of the world.

Everyone will praise him!

His righteousness will be like a garden in early spring, with plants springing up everywhere.

Isaiah 61:1₤11.

Jesus' Good News of God's kingdom.

The beginning of the ministry of Jesus on earth.

After Jesus had been baptised by John (the Baptist), God spoke and said to Him, *"You are my dearly loved Son, and you bring me great joy."*

One day when the crowds were being baptised, Jesus was also baptised.

As he was praying, the Heavens opened, and the Holy Spirit, in bodily form, descended on him like a dove. And a voice from Heaven said, "You are my dearly loved Son, and you bring me great joy."
Luke 3:21-22.

The Spirit of God rested upon Jesus, like a dove.

After this Jesus fasted for forty days in the desert and was tempted by satan but was not overcome.

The scriptures tell us that Jesus then began preaching.

We find some of the words that Jesus spoke, during His ministry on earth, in the gospel of Luke 4:14.

Jesus visited a synagogue to teach.

Jesus stood up in the synagogue and told all who were there that if they prayed the sinner's prayer and put their hands up, they would be assured of a place in Heaven when they die.

Didn't He?

Isn't that what happened?

Well no, strangely enough, it isn't.

What happened, according to scripture, was that Jesus opened the scroll that was handed to Him and read the words of the prophet Isaiah:

"The Spirit of the Lord is upon me, for he has anointed me to bring Good News to the poor. He has sent me to proclaim that captives will be released, that the blind will see, that the oppressed will be set free,
and that the time of the Lord's favour has come."
Isaiah 61:1-2.

Jesus majestically announced the arrival of God's kingdom on earth.

After that day, Jesus taught about nothing but the arrival of God's kingdom; how to gain entrance to it, what the kingdom is and how to live within it.

It is the kingdom that Jesus taught that we will be looking into.

In truth, neither Jesus or His followers ever taught about going to Heaven when we die.

We might have thought that, if the reason that Jesus came to earth was to provide a way for us to go to Heaven when we die, He might have mentioned it while He was here, but we will find that He didn't.

We will look at this popular misconception and the scriptures that are used to promote this misunderstanding.

Disgruntled evangelists and hot headed preachers, you won't have to wait long.

Take five minutes to read and digest Isaiah chapter sixty one at the front of this book.

You will discover that it is filled with promises of a different life for the living on earth, and Isaiah, Jesus and His followers continued to teach how to enter, live in and to build God's kingdom on earth, throughout the scriptures.

It is this kingdom that Jesus taught during His own life here.

Jesus' teaching.

Jesus' most well known period of teaching is recorded in the Gospel of Matthew in chapters five to seven.

Matthew has outlined these in a series of parables, teachings and sayings.

We know them as the sermon on the mount and they include the beatitudes and teaching about being salt and light on the earth.

There is also teaching about the law, anger, adultery, divorce, keeping vows, taking revenge, loving our enemies, giving to those in need, there is teaching about how to pray and fast, how to handle money, possessions and finances, teaching about judging others, how to enter the kingdom, which size gate to use, teaching about fruit - whether we produce bad fruit or good fruit, allowing ourselves to be pruned in order to produce good fruit, teaching about who would be recognised by Jesus as His disciple in the kingdom, who was living in God's kingdom and who was definitely not known by Jesus.

He taught about the types of people who would not be recognised by Jesus when they were asked how they had spent their time on earth at the time of judgement, how to live in God's kingdom, how to be a good disciple and how to build a solid foundation in God's kingdom on earth.

The people were amazed at His teaching, which was outstanding and radical, but most noticeably for us in our study, not a word was taught about going to Heaven when we die.

Everywhere Jesus went He taught about gaining entry to God's kingdom and how to live in God's kingdom on earth.

His disciples realised that Jesus' dynamic and miraculous ministry was centred around His close relationship with His Father and so they asked Jesus how to pray.

Jesus' reply is given in both Matthew and Luke's gospels.

Jesus told His disciples to talk to Father about how to live and within the answer that Jesus gave is some advice to pray to Father about His kingdom becoming established on earth:

May your kingdom come soon. May your will be done on earth, as it is in Heaven.
Matthew 6:10.

Jesus told His disciples to pray about the establishment of God's kingdom on earth - *may the rule of God be on earth, in the same manner as God reigns from Heaven.*

He then went on to tell them more about prayer and how prayer enables the kingdom to come about.

I don't think there can be a genuine argument against the fact that Jesus came to earth in order to announce God's kingdom was at hand, which means that it is at our fingertips - within our reach, and that His death and resurrection enabled all who place their trust in Him to enter the kingdom.

Just in case there are some who are still not sure as to why Jesus came to earth or what His purpose was I will add a few more references.

But he replied, "I must preach the Good News of the kingdom of God in other towns, too, because that is why I was sent."
Luke 4:43.

"The time promised by God has come at last!" he announced. "The kingdom of God is near! Repent of your sins and believe the Good News!"
Mark 1:15.

Soon afterward Jesus began a tour of the nearby towns and villages, preaching and announcing the Good News about the kingdom of God. He took his twelve disciples with him,
Luke 8:1.

Jesus travelled through all the towns and villages of that area, teaching in the synagogues and announcing the Good News about the kingdom. And he healed every kind of disease and illness.
Matthew 9:35.

"If you enter a town and it welcomes you, eat whatever is set before you.
Heal the sick, and tell them, 'The kingdom of God is near you now.'
Luke 10:8-9.

Did you notice that word, 'now'.

Jesus taught that the kingdom of God is accessible now.

There are many more references if we choose to search. The scriptures are full of them.

In truth, the Gospels, the book of The Acts of the Apostles, the letters of the Apostles and the book of Revelation are filled with references to the kingdom of God; what it is made of and instructions on how to build and to live in it on earth.

It is remarkable, given what we are taught today, that nowhere did Jesus say that the good news is that one day we might go to Heaven, after we die.

The good news that Jesus taught appears to be different to the good news that we hear about from many preacher pulpits today.

Believe in the Lord Jesus Christ and you will be saved!

The above words are often written on posters on the side of church buildings or on placards to be paraded on the street.

The advertiser normally intends the words to strike home at unwary passers-by in order to convince them of their need for Jesus.

These are words that have traditionally been used to warn of the threat of an eternity in hell for the person who ignores them.

Where are these words taken from and what do they really mean?

When we look at the events around these words, in the scripture that they are taken from, we will see that they have nothing to do with Heaven or hell or any such thing.

They are words that are given in response to a jailor who was in fear for his life on earth and had nothing to do with eternal damnation.

In the manner in which they are used on billboards - to warn of the threat of hell, they are a deception.

We will look at the story in order to get a better picture.

The events occurred after Jesus had returned to His Father.

Two followers of Jesus, Paul and Silas, had been preaching about the good news of God's kingdom and had been thrown into Jail.

An earthquake occurred whilst they were there and all of the doors broke from their hinges and the chains that held the prisoners were also broken.

Had the prisoners escaped, the jailor, who was responsible for them, would have been executed.

Believing that they had in fact escaped, the jailor was in fear of his life and was about to kill himself with his own sword but when Paul and Silas called out to assure him that they were all still there, the jailor responded with the words, *"what must I do to be saved"?*

In other words, *"what do i have to do so you won't all escape and I will be killed"?*

Paul and Silas then spoke the words that we often see on billboards, *"believe in the Lord Jesus Christ, and you will be saved!"*.

Both the jailor and Paul and Silas were referring to the fact that he was in danger of being executed by the authorities.

The jailer was desperate for hope - for his life.

Paul and Silas offered him security in Jesus.

As a result of these events and the conduct of Paul and Silas, the jailor and his family trusted in Jesus and consequently entered God's kingdom.

Here is the story for you to see for yourself.

Around midnight Paul and Silas were praying and singing hymns to God, and the other prisoners were listening. Suddenly, there was a massive earthquake, and the prison was shaken to its foundations. All the doors immediately flew open, and the chains of every prisoner fell off! The jailer woke up to see the prison doors wide open. He assumed the prisoners had escaped, so he drew his sword to kill himself. But Paul shouted to him, "Stop! Don't kill yourself! We are all here!" The jailer called for lights and ran to the dungeon and fell down trembling before Paul and Silas. Then he brought them out and asked, "Sirs, what must I do to be saved?" They replied, "Believe in the Lord Jesus and you will be saved, along with everyone in your household." And they shared the word of the Lord with him and with all who lived in his household. Even at that hour of the night, the jailer cared for them and washed their wounds.

Then he and everyone in his household were immediately baptised.

Acts of the Apostles 16:25-33.

Why were his household baptised?

So that they too could enter God's kingdom.

We will be looking at what Jesus said about the relationship between baptism and God's kingdom - how to enter God's kingdom and eternal life.

Did anyone read anything about either Heaven or hell within those verses?

I didn't.

Whilst we could extrapolate the story to correctly display the saving power of Jesus generally, we need some other basis to be able to say that this verse is talking about being saved from hell, or being saved to go to Heaven, and there is no basis for such an extrapolation, as we will discover.

Many preachers use the thief on the cross as an example of someone who went straight to Heaven when they died.

Others use the writings about Enoch in the Old Testament and Elijah.

Others use the famed verse in John's Gospel chapter three verse sixteen.

"For this is how God loved the world: He gave his one and only Son, so that everyone who believes in him will not perish but have eternal life.
John 3:16.

We too will look at these examples, and others to understand the truth of Jesus' teaching.

Heaven, God's kingdom and eternal life.

There are several scriptures that have historically been used to promote the promise of going to Heaven when we die.

The first and most well known is found in John's gospel chapter three, verse sixteen.

And as Moses lifted up the bronze snake on a pole in the wilderness, so the Son of Man must be lifted up,
so that everyone who believes in him will have eternal life.

"For this is how God loved the world: He gave his one and only Son, so that everyone who believes in him will not perish but have eternal life.

God sent his Son into the world not to judge the world, but to save the world through him.
John 3:14-17.

I have included a couple of verses on either side in order to give some context.

The words were spoken by Jesus and He was speaking about Himself as the Son of God.

Jesus was talking about the necessity to believe in Him in order to receive eternal life.

He also spoke about the world being saved through Him.

Note that He spoke about receiving eternal life in the present tense but He said nothing about going to Heaven when we die.

There is a distinction that his listeners understood but we don't. We also need to understand.

In order to do so we will look at the full context of why Jesus was saying this.

As we have seen, Jesus spent His life on earth teaching about how to live in God's kingdom.

A Pharisee and member of the Sanhedrin, called Nicodemus, heard about what Jesus was teaching and came to see Him, under cover of darkness, to find out more about this kingdom.

Something of what Jesus was saying had stirred his curiosity.

After dark one evening, he came to speak with Jesus. "Rabbi," he said, "we all know that God has sent you to teach us.
Your miraculous signs are evidence that God is with you."
John 3:2.

Nicodemus had realised that God was with Jesus because of the miracles that He had performed.

The miracles themselves, were an indication that God's kingdom was becoming manifested and Nicodemus recognised that.

Nicodemus wasn't concerned about where he was going when he died, but about God's kingdom, as we can see from the answer that Jesus gave.

Jesus replied, "I tell you the truth, unless you are born again, you cannot see the kingdom of God."
John 3:3.

Jesus began to explain to him what needed to be done in order to gain entry to the kingdom - new birth.

Nicodemus was, understandably, even more confused about this kingdom.

"How can we be born again"? he asked.

Jesus replied, "I assure you, no one can enter the kingdom of God without being born of water and the Spirit.
John 3:5.

Notice that on each occasion that Jesus spoke, He was talking about entry to the kingdom of God in the present tense and not about going to Heaven.

Jesus explained to Nicodemus that entry into the kingdom of God involves water and Spirit - he and we, must be baptised in water to receive the Spirit of God in order to gain entry.

Jesus also told Nicodemus that without being born again in this way, it is impossible to even see the kingdom of God.

Jesus was setting out a principle; faith must come first, then we must act upon that faith by being baptised and then understanding and reality will come to us when we are joined in God's Spirit.

This scripture is often used to preach about going to Heaven when we die, but as we can appreciate it is actually about gaining entry to God's kingdom in the present, on earth.

Jesus does talk about eternal life, which is another aspect of God's kingdom, as we will see, but not about going to Heaven when we die.

Faith.

We have touched briefly on the need for faith.

Faith brings into existence that which previously was not there.

Faith is creative.

The author of the letter to the Hebrews writes about it in this way:

Faith shows the reality of what we hope for; it is the evidence of things we cannot see.
Hebrews 11:1.

Our own faith brings about what we believe to be true.

It is when our faith is transferred into thoughts, words and action that reality is produced.

Faith can work in both a positive and a negative manner.

When we have a negative expectation; faith for bad things to occur, our faith will produce those effects in our lives.

If we have faith in the words of Jesus, who has promised that only good things will be given to His children, we will experience that goodness manifested in our lives too.

The good things may not always be what we might expect.

Father will train and discipline us according to our need, but the end result will be good.

It follows then that if we have faith in a misunderstanding of scripture, our faith has been misguided.

We may have faith in the saving power of Jesus, which is good; Jesus saves.

This is what we call a general faith in the nature of the character of Jesus but is not a specific faith and will not lead us into a new life.

If we are not aware of the kingdom that we are invited into, or the kingdom that we have been saved from, we will not have used our faith in order to enter that kingdom, and if we are not aware of what God's kingdom is, we will not have entered it, even less will we be benefitting from entering it.

There is a need for us to be aware of where we have come from and of where we are going to, in order to enter God's blessings in His kingdom.

Can we be sure of our salvation if we have not entered into an understanding of what salvation is?

We clearly cannot have faith in something we do not know about.

The good news of God's kingdom is not about receiving eternal life when we die but about living in God's kingdom now.

Many have been taught that if they recite the sinner's prayer, their place in Heaven, when they die, will be assured.

This teaching is far from the reality of what Jesus accomplished.

The enemy will continue to keep us in slavery, until we pull down this lie, which is a counterfeit and false gospel.

Until we embrace the truth of God's kingdom we will find it impossible to leave his kingdom of darkness and death.

The enemy has kept many from enjoying the benefits of God's kingdom for so many lost years, down through the centuries.

It is high time that this deceit is overthrown.

The prophet Hosea declared that God's children are being destroyed because they lack knowledge:

'My people are destroyed from lack of knowledge. "Because you have rejected knowledge, I also reject you as my priests; because you have ignored the law of your God, I also will ignore your children'.
Hosea 4:6 NIV

We ignore and reject knowledge at our peril.

Faith used in the battle against the enemy will only be useful if we have an understanding of what we place that faith in.

Don't let your hearts be troubled.

"Don't let your hearts be troubled. Trust in God, and trust also in me.
There is more than enough room in my Father's home. If this were not so, would I have told you that I am going to prepare a place for you?
When everything is ready, I will come and get you, so that you will always be with me where I am.
John 14:1-3.

On the face of it this must definitely be Jesus telling His followers about going to Heaven to be with Him when they die, isn't it?

When we read the full discourse we discover that Jesus is talking about the expansiveness of His Father.

Jesus told His disciples four times in this conversation that they will be with Him while they are alive, on earth.

No, I will not abandon you as orphans - I will come to you.
John 14:18.

When I am raised to life again, you will know that I am in my Father, and you are in me, and I am in you.
John 14:20.

Jesus replied, "All who love me will do what I say. My Father will love them, and we will come and make our home with each of them.
John 14:23.

Remember what I told you: I am going away, but I will come back to you again.
John 14:28.

Jesus was telling them that He will return to them and they will be one with Him and one with The Father, not after they had died but whilst they were alive.

In the first three verses above Jesus was talking about His Fathers house, how big and inclusive it is.

God's house, or God's mansion, as some versions have translated it - *"in my Father's mansion" kjv,* is another way of talking about God's temple.

There are places, or responsibilities, in that house that are already prepared for them, and us.

Jesus was talking about the inclusiveness of the Father's kingdom and the fact that there is room for the disciples to live there with Jesus.

Jesus was talking about the present and not an afterlife.

He was telling them that He will take them to Himself, to be one with them and with the Father, whilst they are alive.

Paul wrote to the Ephesian Christians about a similar theme:

For we are God's masterpiece. He has created us anew in Christ Jesus, so we can do the good things he planned for us long ago.
Ephesians 2:10.

When Jesus was talking about preparing a place for them, and us, He was telling them that they have responsibilities and a purpose in building God's kingdom on earth.

The disciples had already been taught about building God's kingdom on earth and so understood the context.

Jesus had told them to pray, *'may your kingdom come, may your will be done, on earth…*

Elsewhere in scripture we read about the gift of eternal life.

We will look at the reality of receiving that gift of eternal life, but we will discover that eternal life and going to Heaven when we die are not the same thing.

Am I suggesting that Heaven does not exist?

Not at all.

Where is Heaven?

This is what the Lord says: "Heaven is my throne, and the earth is my footstool. Could you build me a temple as good as that? Could you build me such a resting place?
Isaiah 66:1.

The prophet Isaiah described Heaven as the throne of God.

We tend to arrive at our impressions of Heaven from what we have been presented by Hollywood or from watching our televisions and from preachers who have been misinformed.

These images are deceitful at best.

We know from scripture that God lives in Heaven:

then hear their prayers and their petition from Heaven where you live, and uphold their cause.
1 Kings 8:49.

Jesus said,
Pray like this: Our Father in Heaven, may your name be kept holy.
Matthew 6:9.

We also know from scripture that God lives amongst His people:

Don't you realise that all of you together are the temple of God and that the Spirit of God lives in you?
1 Corinthians 3:16.

God lives in Heaven and God also lives among His people.

They are the same place.

Heaven describes the realm that God governs from.

God governs through His people.

As we have read, it is His throne.

We understand Heaven as being an area that God inhabits, but in our minds we have the understanding reversed.

God is not restricted by an area we might call Heaven.

Heaven - His glory, surrounds the area where God is.

To put it another way, Heaven is where God's influence exists.

When we exercise our responsibility in the restoration of God's creation on earth, in bringing all things under His feet, we extend the area of God's government, which in turn allows God, and necessarily Heaven, into that area - the invisible realm of Heaven is being brought to earth by the fact that we are using His authority..

Despite what we see, in the art galleries, of scenes of God sitting amongst the clouds, encircled by angels, in truth, God is Spirit and invisible.

As He is invisible, God doesn't require a physical area to dwell in.

There is not a physical area that could contain the glory that is God.

And yet the Bible describes Heaven as being the place where God lives.

The prophet Elijah described Heaven as a place where God sent fire from:

But Elijah replied to the captain, "If I am a man of God, let fire come down from Heaven and destroy you and your fifty men!" Then fire fell from Heaven and killed them all.
2 Kings 1:10.

Heaven is clearly a place that we cannot see or imagine unless we have spiritual eyes, and yet God lives there, angels are dispatched from there and real fire falls from there.

Stephen, who was a follower of Jesus, looked into Heaven as he was being stoned to death.

But Stephen, full of the Holy Spirit, gazed steadily into Heaven and saw the glory of God, and he saw Jesus standing in the place of honour at God's right hand.
Acts of the Apostles 7:55.

The reason that Stephen was able to look into Heaven has to do with the fact that he was full of God's Spirit.

The reason that many of us are unable to perceive Heaven is that we tend to be very full of ourselves and extremely low on God's Spirit.

Heaven is generally an invisible, spiritual realm that we don't access.

I do not say that we can't access Heaven - the scriptures advise to the contrary, but we tend not to.

When we learn to dispose of our fleshly self and allow God to rise up in us we will find Heaven becoming an increasing reality for us.

Notice that Stephen didn't say that he looked into God's kingdom. Stephen was already living in God's kingdom but he looked into Heaven.

Stephen and Luke, the author of the acts of the Apostles, understood the difference.

Whilst Heaven is an invisible realm for unspiritual people - those who have not been restored through Jesus, it is clearly visible for those who are full of the Spirit of God and for the fallen spirits who live in opposition to God.

One day the members of the Heavenly court came to present themselves before the Lord, and the Accuser, Satan, came with them.
Job 1:6.

Satan, and other fallen angels, are aware of Heaven.

Paul who wrote many of the letters that we find in the Bible, visited Heaven:

I was caught up to the third Heaven fourteen years ago. Whether I was in my body or out of my body, I don't know - only God knows.
Yes, only God knows whether I was in my body or outside my body.
But I do know that I was caught up to paradise and heard things so astounding that they cannot be expressed in words, things no human is allowed to tell.
2 Corinthians 12:2-4.

We can also read in the book of Revelation that John, a disciple of Jesus, was worshipping in the Spirit when he was taken into Heaven, to be given several visions.

Heaven is open for those who take Jesus at His word and are filled with Spirit.

Heaven - the abode of God, is a realm we can access if and when we take Jesus at his word.

Jesus replied, "All who love me will do what I say. My Father will love them, and we will come and make our home with each of them.
John 14:23.

Now all of us can come to the Father through the same Holy Spirit because of what Christ has done for us.
Ephesians 2:18.

Through him you Gentiles are also being made part of this dwelling where God lives by his Spirit.
Ephesians 2:22.

During the period of the Old Testament God dwelt with the children of Israel inside a tent that was known as the Holy of Holies.

Only the chief priest was ever allowed to go behind the big heavy curtain that hid the Holy of Holies and just once each year, on *'Yom Kippur',* after much preparation, sacrifice and purification.

Ordinary sinful people were not allowed near God.

When Jesus gave His life on the cross, His unselfish act of love removed the obstacle that had kept us from meeting with God personally - our sin was dealt with forever.

In a symbolic gesture which confirmed the fact that we are now able to access God in the Holy of Holies, the physical curtain, that had separated the people in the temple from God, was torn from top to bottom.

At that moment the curtain in the sanctuary of the Temple was torn in two, from top to bottom. The earth shook, rocks split apart,
Matthew 27:51.

Once, we were not able to come near to God but as a consequence of what Jesus achieved, Heaven - the invisible dwelling place of God, can now be accessed by any of us, through Jesus.

We are able to come and go, to and from Heaven - into the presence of God.

In truth, God's desire is for us to dwell in His presence permanently.

It is only our immaturity that prevents us from living in the presence of God all of the time.

This situation will change as we move increasingly into the age of God's kingdom.

Now we flit in and out like moths around a bright light, but as we grow in the love of Jesus we will learn to spend increasingly more time with Him and our walk will not be one of our own but one lived in unity with Him.

But neither Jesus or any of His followers suggested that Heaven is a place we go to when we die, for good reason.

The reason has to do with the nature, make-up and existence of the kingdom of God.

God's kingdom.

We have seen that Jesus taught about living in God's kingdom in the present, contrary to the popular belief that He taught about going to Heaven when we die.

We know also that Jesus offered eternal life:

"For this is how God loved the world: He gave his one and only Son, so that everyone who believes in him will not perish but have eternal life.
John 3:16.

There appears to be a conflict in what I am suggesting about not going to Heaven when we die.

Those who heard Jesus' words understood what He was saying but we have been sold a different story and in order for us to understand we need to get a clear picture of what the kingdom that Jesus brought into being is.

God's kingdom is an eternal kingdom.

It is not of this world but we live in it on earth.

It is a spiritual kingdom, built upon spiritual principles and is expressed by the manner in which we live on earth.

Jesus taught how to live in His kingdom and He sent God's Spirit to teach us further and to enable us to live in that way.

God's kingdom has to do with the way we conduct our relationships with each other.

God's kingdom has a foundation that is love - God is love.

Whilst we live in the kingdom of darkness - satan's kingdom of death, we are unable to live in love but when we enter God's kingdom, through baptism, we receive God's Spirit - we become one with Him and then He enables us to live our lives in love.

This is the transition that Jesus talked to Nicodemus about.

Jesus replied, "I assure you, no one can enter the kingdom of God without being born of water and the Spirit.
John 3:5.

When we live in God's kingdom we learn to clothe ourselves with Christ.

Instead, clothe yourself with the presence of the Lord Jesus Christ. And don't let yourself think about ways to indulge your evil desires.
Romans 13:14.

This is another way of describing the changed way of living that we take on through our unity with Jesus - with God.

By living in relationship with others in this new way - love, we reveal God's kingdom on earth.

As we grow, mature, discover Jesus and begin to become like Him, we will be given further responsibilities.

We will learn how to overcome the consequences of sin - the darkness that has reigned on the earth for so many years.

We can learn how to bring restoration to the earth - God's creation.

The powers of darkness that rule people's lives can be broken; people can be set free.

The declaration that Jesus made through the words that we read about at the beginning of this book will be continued and expanded upon.

"The Spirit of The Lord is upon me, because He has anointed me to preach Good News!"

God's kingdom will become established on earth.

By building God's kingdom on earth in this manner, Jesus will be seen among us.

We will reflect Him in our lives.

Jesus will appear on earth.

When we begin to live in love, in true, loving relationships with others; when we learn to bring restoration to God's creation; when the world begins to see God's kingdom appear on the earth, Jesus will, in truth, come, with His Father, to live with us.

Jesus will return to reign in His kingdom as He promised that He would.

"Men of Galilee," they said, "why are you standing here staring into Heaven? Jesus has been taken from you into Heaven, but someday he will return from Heaven in the same way you saw him go!"
Acts of the Apostles 1:11.

The men, or angels who were present when Jesus went into the cloud told the disciples that Jesus will come to earth to reign, in the same way that the disciples saw Him go.

How did Jesus go?

He entered the presence of God - He entered the cloud, which is another way of describing God's presence.

The angel said that He would return in the same way.

That must mean that Jesus will return out of the presence of God - God's dwelling place.

Where is God's dwelling place?

God lives within His people.

For we are the temple of the living God. As God said: "I will live in them and walk among them. I will be their God, and they will be my people.
2 Corinthians 6:16.

So, that must mean that when Jesus returns, He will be returning from out of God's temple - us.

When we, the people of God, learn to dwell in the presence of God in righteousness, in His kingdom, He will live among us, we will reflect him to the world and Jesus will return to reign, from out of that very presence of God, among us.

Heaven - the presence of God, will accompany Him.

Heaven is not a place that we go to when we die.

Heaven will dwell with us on earth.

We will learn to live in the presence of God.

Jesus did not teach about our going to Heaven when we die, but when He returns, as we learn to clothe ourselves with Him, by living in righteousness and by learning to overcome the enemy, who attempts to prevent that kingdom, He will be bringing Heaven to earth.

In truth, the wider and deeper that God's kingdom is established on earth in our lives, the more we will experience Heaven.

Jesus taught His disciples to pray towards this end like this:

"Father, may your kingdom come, may your will be done, on earth...."
Matt 6:10 and Luke 11:2.

What is it like to live in God's presence?

We have all been given different ideas about what going to Heaven will be like, often from corrupt sources, such as historical myths, film or television, comic books and even teachers of scripture.

It is often better for us to close our minds from these influences and to hear what God is saying to us instead, by reading the Bible and listening to Him.

We can discover what living in His kingdom is like by learning from His example and by looking at how others live in His kingdom.

Jesus lived within God's presence, He certainly lived in His kingdom.

That kingdom was demonstrated by his character, words, deeds and lifestyle.

Jesus went to bed at night, He rose in the morning and dressed.

He will have washed the dishes and He might even have put out the cat.

The first man and woman also lived in God's presence - in harmony with God.

They had a vast tract of land to manage.

They found their work and lives enjoyable because there was no influence from sin.

There were four great rivers running through that land.

They had the care of wild and domestic animals, fish, birds and small furry animals, that scurried along the ground.

They worked on forestry, collecting food and managing their surroundings.

They lived a life much as we do, but without the influence or effect of sin.

We sometimes say to ourselves things like, "it would be Heaven if I didn't have to get up every morning".

Or, "wouldn't it be nice if I had all the money I needed".

Our thoughts are motivated by fear, greed, selfishness, lust and, self.

Living without those thoughts that emanate from living in a sinful environment, which is the realm of satan, our thoughts and motivations will be very different.

We are sold the idea that being in Heaven is having all that we desire or lying on a sunbed being waited on by angels.

We will discover that living in God's kingdom without the effects of sin, that are upon creation at present, will be a very different experience.

We will discover we have all that we need already.

We will discover that we don't envy or desire what others have.

We will have learnt that we don't need to quarrel or argue about anything.

We will find pleasure in everything around us.

We will enjoy the work that we have.

Our lives will be satisfying and fulfilled.

Our motivations will alter.

The daily battles that seek to bring us down, will be easily overcome, as we learn to listen to Jesus.

Sin will be excluded from our lives.

We may well find that we still put the cat out at night and wash the dishes.

We were designed to live in the creation that God brought into being.

John Lennon sang a song called Imagine but he didn't really have any concept of the reality of his words.

We find it difficult to imagine a life without the consequences of sin but this is the reality of what Jesus has achieved and the life that we are entering when we come into God's kingdom.

We live within that life by overcoming the enemy that attempts to tempt us to think bad thoughts and say and do things that are harmful for us and those around us.

We are not kind, but by overcoming our weaknesses, we will learn to love.

It is a kingdom that has many victories to come in overcoming the enemy, but the battles have already been won.

It is a kingdom that is ours to receive.

We might reply that we don't and can't live in that way because the consequences of sin are all around us.

Our own lives are not righteous and we tend to think, say and do, things that are not good.

We have been sold the lie that we are as we are, and we are unable to change.

However, the truth is that Jesus overcame the enemy completely when He voluntarily gave up His life, died and rose again from the dead.

The enemy, who is satan, has told us that we can't change, but this is not true.

He has been overcome and is a defeated enemy.

We need to learn to listen to the truth and ignore the lies.

We have the ability now to rid ourselves of sin and the influence of satan.

We can learn to forgive others.

It is not too hard when we appreciate what forgiveness we have been given.

It is not too hard for us when we realise that Jesus has already won the battles on our behalf.

Addictive habits can be removed with a word.

Harmful thoughts can be disposed of forever.

The spirit of negativity, laziness, apathy and lethargy can be exposed and banished.

Spirits of envy and deviousness can be disposed of.

Jesus sent God's Spirit to help us to overcome the enemy and we can learn to become kind; we can learn to love.

When we walk into God's kingdom, God's Spirit will begin to renew our mind and to teach us how to live - how to overcome.

The reason that Jesus went back to His Father was for that very purpose.

He is patiently awaiting the building and establishment of His kingdom on earth.

That is a job that must be accomplished by us in order for us to be trained in battle.

Our job is not to sit around waiting to die to be transported to Heaven, but to establish God's kingdom on earth so that Jesus can return and reign.

We have The Spirit of the living God with us to teach us how to live; how to overcome.

The Spirit is not here to help us struggle through to our dying day; struggling isn't what we are born for, but to teach us how to become a righteous, victorious people who are living in a loving relationship with each other, in unity.

The lie that tells us that all we need to do is wait until we die and then be transported to Heaven, has severely hampered the building of that kingdom.

We have become focussed on our lives, how long will we live? our comfort, our wellbeing, our prosperity.

Our questions have been, are we good enough to get into Heaven? Is our place secure? Are we doing enough?

Heaven has become the idol that we worship.

If we live in that way we might find that we never inherit the kingdom that Jesus died for us to have.

It is high time that the lie is silenced.

After two thousand years of wandering in darkness there is a dying need for our focus to be on the teachings of Jesus - on building God's kingdom on earth.

Eternity.

We can see that Jesus' purpose wasn't to transport people to Heaven when they die, but for us to build an eternal kingdom to prepare for Heaven to come to earth.

When Jesus returns, those who have entered His kingdom, lived an overcoming life, and have died, will be raised from death and given a new spiritual body.

Paul wrote about this in a letter to the Corinthians:

But someone may ask, "How will the dead be raised? What kind of bodies will they have?"

What a foolish question! When you put a seed into the ground, it doesn't grow into a plant unless it dies first. And what you put in the ground is not the plant that will grow, but only a bare seed of wheat or whatever you are planting.

Then God gives it the new body he wants it to have. A different plant grows from each kind of seed.

It is the same way with the resurrection of the dead. Our earthly bodies are planted in the ground when we die, but they will be raised to live forever.
1 Corinthians 15:35-42.

He went on to describe that transformation:

What I am saying, dear brothers and sisters, is that our physical bodies cannot inherit the kingdom of God.

These dying bodies cannot inherit what will last forever. But let me reveal to you a wonderful secret. We will not all die, but we will all be transformed!

It will happen in a moment, in the blink of an eye, when the last trumpet is blown. For when the trumpet sounds, those who have died will be raised to live forever. And we who are living will also be transformed.
1 Corinthians 15:50-52.

Jesus said:

"I tell you the truth, those who listen to my message and believe in God who sent me have eternal life.

They will never be condemned for their sins, but they have already passed from death into life.
John 5:24.

Those who listen and believe have already passed from death into life.

My sheep listen to my voice; I know them, and they follow me.

I give them eternal life, and they will never perish. No one can snatch them away from me,
John 10:27-28.

Jesus was talking about people who listen to Him and respond to Him, not once, but continually.

He didn't say they will have eternal life one day when they die but, *"I give them eternal life and they will never perish"*.

Jesus spoke in the present tense.

Eternal life for those who listen and respond to Jesus begins in this life.

Jesus talked about eternal life almost as often as he taught about God's kingdom; the two subjects are intertwined.

When we enter God's kingdom in this life we immediately receive eternal life because death no longer has any claim on us.

The thief on the cross.

I have heard many preachers speak about the people who are already living in Heaven.

The thief who died with Jesus on the cross is a notable example.

So, let's look at this event to discover if what we have been told can be true.

There were two others who were crucified with Jesus, one on either side of Him.

One of the men mocked Jesus, the other, who was a thief, realised who Jesus was and asked to be remembered when Jesus came back to His kingdom.

Matthew, Mark and Luke all record the incident:

Then he said, "Jesus, remember me when you come into your kingdom."

And Jesus replied, "I assure you, today you will be with me in paradise."
Luke 23:42-43.

It appears that the thief was aware of Jesus' teaching.

In fact Matthew records that both of these criminals were mocking Jesus initially, so it is likely that Jesus, even whilst they were being crucified, during the three hours of darkness, had spent some time talking to the thief about God's kingdom.

The thief then asked to be remembered when Jesus returned to His kingdom.

According to our Bibles, Jesus gave a solemn promise to the thief that, yes, indeed, he would be with Jesus in His kingdom that day. *(paradise)*.

Or did He?

Some might not realise that the original scriptures did not have verse numbers, chapter headings, subtitles or punctuation - full stops, commas, colons, semi-colons, paragraphs, etc.

The translators of scripture have inserted those as they see fit according to their own understanding of the documents.

Like many today, the translators had little understanding of God's kingdom on earth and had been taught that Heaven was our destination.

They have therefore ignored the normal manner of Jesus' speech and placed a comma in the sentence in order for the words of Jesus to read, *"today you will be with me in paradise"*.

In truth, Jesus is extremely unlikely to have told the thief this, as Jesus wasn't in Heaven to meet him in paradise that day.

It was to be at least three days, and probably forty days, before Jesus returned to His Father, and Jesus wasn't one to mislead.

Jesus told Mary that very thing at the tomb:

"Don't cling to me," Jesus said, *"for I haven't yet ascended to the Father.*
John 20:17.

When we look at what the thief asked Jesus - to be remembered when Jesus returned to His kingdom, we can see that it is even more unlikely that Jesus would have given him the reply *"today you will be with me in paradise"*.

The answer didn't reply to the question.

Jesus' manner of speech is well noted throughout the four gospels.

We can read over sixty six times that Jesus used the phrase, *'verily verily, I say unto you"* or "truly, truly, I tell you".

This is the same phrase as, *"I tell you today,"*.

When we consider the speech pattern of Jesus, combined with the question that the thief asked and the fact that Jesus wasn't in paradise on that day to meet the thief, we can see that the more likely words of Jesus are, *"I tell you today, you will be with me in paradise"*.

We have moved the comma one word along the sentence in order to make sense of Jesus' reply.

It is unlikely that Jesus told the thief that he would be with Him that day in Heaven, (He wasn't there), but that he would be remembered - raised up from the dead, in God's kingdom when Jesus returned.

Punctuation can make the difference between life and death and this probable error on behalf of our translators of scripture has enabled the enemy to deceive many through the ages.

I will give you another example of punctuation error.

Let's eat Grandma!

Let's eat, Grandma!

We can see for ourselves how our own beliefs might impact on the understanding of a text that had no punctuation whatsoever.

We can assume that the thief is still waiting for his resurrection, when Jesus returns to His kingdom.

Enoch.

I have talked a little about Enoch, the father of Methuselah and the great grandfather of Noah, in my commentary on the book of Genesis part one.

Let us look at it again here.

Preachers often use Enoch as being an example of those who are alive in Heaven.

But was his experience of being transported to Heaven as we have been led to believe?

All the information we have with regards to Enoch is a few short sentences in the Bible.

After the birth of Methuselah, Enoch lived in close fellowship with God for another 300 years, and he had other sons and daughters.

Enoch lived 365 years walking in close fellowship with God. Then one day he disappeared, because God took him.
Genesis 5:22-24.

We must take some time to analyse what we know of his life and passing because what we believe of Enoch will affect our understanding of Heaven, eternal life, the kingdom of God, and our own foundation of faith.

The writer to the Hebrews, when talking about people of faith, tells us that.

'It was by faith that Enoch was taken up to Heaven without dying - "he disappeared, because God took him."
For before he was taken up, he was known as a person who pleased God'.
Hebrews 11:5.

The same writer to the Hebrews uses a similar idea when describing king Melchizedec.

Because there are no details of Mechizedek's birth or death in scripture, the writer used Melchizedek in a symbolic way, as a man who *lived forever.*
Hebrews. 7:13-17.

It is likely that, in a similar manner, the writer to the Hebrews took the same verse that we have in Genesis, with regards to Enoch *not being found,* and expanded it to use Enoch as an example of the reward for *living in faith* and declared that, *he was taken to Heaven.*

I do not say that Enoch didn't spend much time in God's presence in Heaven, as many others have whilst still alive.

The question is rather, was Enoch taken to Heaven after he died?

The declaration of the writer of the letter to the Hebrews is not found elsewhere in scripture.

We know from our verse in Genesis chapter five that Enoch was a righteous man and he walked with God.

The only other thing that we know for sure is that *he couldn't be found.*

We are told that *God took him.*

The fact that Enoch disappeared and *couldn't be found,* implies that people were looking for him.

There is another incident where a person was taken up into the sky and couldn't be found, although many people looked for him.

This was when the prophet Elijah was taken up into the sky by a fiery chariot at the end of his ministry. *2. Kings. 2:11.*

He had just handed over his cloak to Elisha, who was to take his place, and all those around saw him taken away in this manner.

Elisha told the people around not to go looking for him, but they did anyway, in case he had been dropped on a nearby mountain, but they couldn't find him.

The prophets, who were his students, clearly had no thought that he had been taken to Heaven.

It has often been assumed that he too was taken into Heaven, but when we study scripture further we find that ten years after this incident, while he was still ministering, he wrote a letter to king Jehoram.
2 Chronicles 21:12.

It is doubtful that Elijah wrote the letter from Heaven, but that he was still alive - God had taken him to a place where Elisha, would not be overshadowed by the presence of his predecessor.

The death of Moses is another incident that involved a supernatural burial, similar to that of Enoch's.

Moses misrepresented God when leading the Israelites through the desert and as a consequence, although he was a man who *walked with God,* he was not allowed to enter the land that the Israelites inherited, but was allowed to stand on the top of a mountain to view the land from a distance.

Afterwards God *took him* and buried him on Mount Nebo.

There were no humans at the burial of Moses.

The place was kept secret, presumably because God didn't want his place of death to become a shrine, as had the cave of Machpelah where Abraham and his family were buried and the tomb where Rachael, Jacob's wife, was buried.

There has never been another prophet in Israel like Moses, whom the Lord knew face to face.
Deuteronomy 34:10.

Both of these men walked with God, as we have heard that Enoch did, and after they were *taken away by God*, they were *not to be found.*

Only God and the angels knew where they were.

We have no knowledge of the burial place of either Moses or Elijah.

In the same way as in the passing of Enoch, they were not to be found, because God took them.

Enoch was a righteous man who walked with God.

His life span was extremely short in comparison to those who went before and came after.

He lived just three hundred and sixty five years, that we know about.

If he was taken into Heaven, (he may be the only one, I will not argue the point), but scripture doesn't tell us that.

It is difficult to make precise and definite judgments upon a text that existed several thousand years ago and was written in a language, about which very little is known.

The manner of his disappearance may have been noteworthy, but we are not given any details of this, apart from the symbolic writing of the author of the letter to the Hebrews who also used the symbolism that Melchizedec lived forever.

Enoch was a righteous man who no doubt spent much time *walking with God* in the Heavenlies.

It is possible, and even likely, that his place of burial was concealed, as Moses was, by God.

It is also likely that God transported him to another place, as was the case with Elijah, perhaps because he was being persecuted for his trust in God.

We simply do not know.

I have heard many preachers talk about the fact that there are two men in Heaven as well as Jesus - Elijah and Enoch.

Whilst this might be the case, it is unlikely.

I don't see any reason why they would be with God in that way, I have found no evidence in scripture to support that they are, and much evidence to suggest that they are not.

There have been many who have been raised from the dead only to die again, but in truth Paul made it very clear that there are none besides Jesus who have been raised to eternity.

He wrote to the Corinthians about this very issue:

But in fact, Christ has been raised from the dead. He is the first of a great harvest of all who have died.

But there is an order to this resurrection: Christ was raised as the first of the harvest; then all who belong to Christ will be raised when he comes back.
1 Corinthians 15:20, 23.

If Christ was the first fruit of the harvest, as Paul tells us that He was, how can there be others who have gone before?

In truth, Paul goes further and declares that, *'all who belong to Christ will be raised when He comes back'.*

What we understand of Heaven has an impact on what expectations we have with regards to our responsibility and rewards in building God's kingdom, and the return of Jesus, to reign on earth.

Paul realised that none of those who had died would have gone to Heaven because he wrote to Timothy about the same problem:

This kind of talk spreads like cancer, as in the case of Hymenaeus and Philetus.

They have left the path of truth, claiming that the resurrection of the dead has already occurred; in this way, they have turned some people away from the faith. 2 Timothy 2:17-18.

Had Paul believed that anyone had gone to Heaven when they died he would not have told Timothy to beware of those who teach such things.

The resurrection of the dead had not occurred during Paul's time and it has not occurred since.

Peter, one of Jesus' closest disciples, said of king David:

For David himself never ascended into Heaven, yet he said, 'The Lord said to my Lord, "Sit in the place of honour at my right hand
Acts of the Apostles 2:34.

Had Peter believed in a resurrection to Heaven he would be sure to believe that king David had been one of those who had been resurrected.

We too can be sure that, despite what popular folklore dictates, our loved ones are not looking down on us from Heaven and, as Paul confirmed, *'neither are any yet resurrected'*.

We must wait for the return of Jesus.

How long must we wait?

The return of Jesus is dependent upon how long the bride of the groom takes to adorn herself with robes of righteousness.

The Groom is waiting for the Bride.

Are we working towards that goal?

Will we be among the ones who are the bride, reigning with Jesus?

Restoring the faith.

Let's look again at what Paul wrote to Timothy:

They have left the path of truth, claiming that the resurrection of the dead has already occurred; in this way, they have turned some people away from the faith.
2 Timothy 2:18.

Paul took the claim that the resurrection had already occurred very seriously.

In fact he went as far as to say that it turned people away from the faith - it is a teaching that is opposed to the truth of the good news of the kingdom.

In the light of what we now know about God's kingdom becoming established on earth we can perhaps understand why.

Jesus spoke about these times:

And many false prophets will appear and will deceive many people.
Matthew 24:11.

Paul also wrote to the Galatian followers in this way:

You are following a different way that pretends to be the Good News but is not the Good News at all.

You are being fooled by those who deliberately twist the truth concerning Christ.

Let God's curse fall on anyone, including us or even an angel from Heaven, who preaches a different kind of Good News than the one we preached to you.

I say again what we have said before: If anyone preaches any other Good News than the one you welcomed, let that person be cursed.
Galatians 1:6-9.

God's curse will be upon all who preach a different good news, to the good news of God's kingdom.

As we have seen from Paul's letter to Timothy there were those who were proposing that the resurrection had already occurred in those early days.

There are those who preach a false gospel with regards to Heaven and the kingdom of God today.

Paul warned that this heresy would spread like gangrene.

Philetus, Alexandra and Hymenaeus were part of a group of people who were introducing these, and other heresies, and because of this heretical teaching were excluded from the fellowship of the believers in Ephesus at the time of Paul's writing.

The idea of being transported to a place of idyl at the point of death was of Greek origin and was an idea readily taken up by some who should have known better.

The Emperor Constantine seized on this same idea during the fourth century a.d. and incorporated it within the counterfeit world religion that he set up, in opposition to the people of the way, which is the manner in which Christians were widely recognised then.

The same heretical doctrine has been used by the Catholic Bishops, priests and clergy, who inherited the false religion that Constantine began.

They found it to be a useful tool in keeping a hand of power over the population, by warning of the loss of their entry to Heaven if they didn't tow the line, in various ways.

Sadly, there has been little revelation or change over the centuries, although God has given some revelation to some individuals, such as Martin Luther, and various protestant groups and their consequent offshoots with regards to other truths.

The darkness, which has been a consequence of Constantine's false doctrines, has remained among the religious, denominational groupings to this day and are still widely taught the world over.

Jesus spoke about the people who refuse to listen to the quiet whisper of God's Spirit.

"Not everyone who calls out to me, 'Lord! Lord!' will enter the kingdom of Heaven. Only those who actually do the will of my Father in Heaven will enter.

On judgement day many will say to me, 'Lord! Lord! We prophesied in your name and cast out demons in your name and performed many miracles in your name.'

But I will reply, 'I never knew you. Get away from me, you who break God's laws.'
Matthew 7:21-23.

Many of us are unable to hear the voice of God because we don't listen; we love the security that denomination and doctrine provides; we live in rebellion, doing what we might believe is the will of God, gaining approbation from our peers, building personal empires, in terms of numbers that follow us, but in truth, pleasing ourselves.

If we do not want to hear the words of Jesus, *"depart from me, I never knew you"* we might not want to continue in that way.

The Lord is restoring truth to those who hear His voice and who respond to Him at this time.

There are others who will continue in their own strength, under their own ability, using their own understanding, and ignore that voice.

The rapture.

I have discussed the doctrine of the rapture in my book, The Shaking.

I will open it up again and expand on it here.

The doctrine with regards to a rapture of God's children is a very similar misunderstanding of scripture to that of departing to Heaven when we die.

We can see that it follows the same thread - a belief that we will be taken away from earth; the place that God created for us to enjoy with Him.

The proposal is that at some point in the future all Christians will be transported to Heaven in order to save them from the forces of evil that are threatening to overpower us.

From what we have discovered of the kingdom of God being established on earth and the fact that the enemy has already been overcome and that it is our responsibility to further expand God's kingdom on earth, we might realise that the doctrine must be incorrect, but many still cling to it and so we will carefully dismantle it here.

It is another ploy of the enemy that seeks to divert our attention from building God's kingdom on earth.

Why, if we are wandering around with our heads in the air, looking at the clouds above, waiting to be whisked away, would we be in the least bit interested in building the kingdom that Jesus taught His followers about?

The enemy continues to attempt to disrupt God's purposes.

The supposition that Christians would be taken away from the earth at some unknown point in time, was a heresy made popular in the church by a man named John Nelson Darby, who lived from 1800 to 1882.

He was born in Ireland and, with others, initiated the Brethren denomination.

He was subsequently involved in the exclusive Brethren, when there was a division in that denomination.

The idea of a rapture was, quite rightly, strongly opposed by Charles Spurgeon, who lived during the same era.

However, this teaching has caught on amongst many Christian groups and has spread far and wide, particularly among American evangelicals.

We have looked at some of these issues earlier but it won't hurt to go over them again from a slightly different angle.

In order to discuss the rapture we need to think about Heaven - where and what it is.

Is it a place that exists in the sky somewhere?

Does Heaven have a geographical identity above our atmosphere or in the solar system?

Or does Heaven - the place where God lives, exist in another realm?

"Where is Heaven"? is a question that has been asked by many, for different reasons.

Scripture gives us some clues.

Jesus seems to indicate that it is a place that is very close to us.

You won't be able to say, 'Here it is!' or 'It's over there!' For the kingdom of God is already among you."
Luke 17:21.

If Heaven - the abode of God, is among us, how could it also be a place that we can be transported to?

In the book of Acts we read that Stephen looked into Heaven.

But Stephen, full of the Holy Spirit, gazed steadily into Heaven and saw the glory of God, and he saw Jesus standing in the place of honour at God's right hand.
Acts of the Apostles 7:55.

Paul was also temporarily taken into Heaven:

I was caught up to the third Heaven fourteen years ago. Whether I was in my body or out of my body, I don't know—only God knows.
2 Corinthians 12:2.

John was also shown visions in Heaven:

And instantly I was in the Spirit, and I saw a throne in Heaven and someone sitting on it.
Revelation 4:2.

As we have discussed previously, Heaven isn't far away from us at all.

In truth, we are able to come and go, to and from Heaven.

We will need to bear this in mind as we look at this issue.

The word rapture - *'rapere'* is latin in origin.

It is taken from the Greek word, *'harpagēsometha'*, which appears only once in the original scriptures, in 1

Thessalonians, 4.17 of our Bibles, and means to be caught up, snatched or seized.

This is the only instance in scripture that we have anything, that is even vaguely, a reference to being taken away.

The idea of a rapture has its roots in a misunderstanding of something that Paul was explaining to the Thessalonian Christians:

For the Lord himself will come down from Heaven with a commanding shout, with the voice of the archangel, and with the trumpet call of God. First, the believers who have died will rise from their graves.

Then, together with them, we who are still alive and remain on the earth will be caught up in the clouds to meet the Lord in the air. Then we will be with the Lord forever.
1 Thessalonians 4:16-17.

Paul was writing about being caught up when the Lord returns in the clouds, which is another way of talking about Heaven.

Paul was explaining to the Christians that when the Lord returns, the dead in Christ will rise first, and will be transformed from death into life.

We will all then meet Jesus in the air.

It is the phrase, in the air, that has caused some trouble.

So let's look at both of these phrases.

Firstly to be caught up - *'Rapere'* in Latin and *'harpagēsometha',* in Greek.

Paul was describing the act of being one with Jesus.

We will be gathered to Him - snatched away not to another place, but from whatever we are doing at that time.

We will be caught up in the wonderment that is Jesus.

Heaven will accompany Jesus, as it is the abode of God.

Jesus will appear from Heaven; which is where God lives; *in our midst.*

We will be enthralled by His presence and overtaken by it.

Jesus will be on centre stage.

Therefore we will all be seized by that scene. All of which is incorporated in that word *'rapere'.*

Paul is not describing being taken from the earth.

Indeed it might be strange that he would, as Jesus will have just returned to it, to claim His kingdom, as He promised His disciples that He would.

Paul is talking about being taken up by His presence.

Another word in discussion is the phrase in the air.

As many Christians will have been buried for an unknown period of time it needs no explanation as to why Paul writes *in the air* on their behalf, but he is also alluding to the fact that we will be in the earth's atmosphere and not somewhere else.

In truth Paul is describing Jesus appearing on earth, having come from another realm - Heaven, bringing Heaven to earth and not vice versa.

Paul was telling the Thessalonians that we will all be on earth, the dead and the living, in the earth's atmosphere (air), together with Jesus.

It is thought that the Thessalonian Christians had been told incorrectly, that Jesus had already returned and that they had missed the event.

Paul was giving an answer to that misunderstanding.

Let us too spread the truth in order to dismantle those thoughts and doctrines that distract us from the purposes of God.

We have looked at what Paul said about those who preach a different gospel.

The good news of God's kingdom.

We have discovered, I think quite conclusively, that the good news of God's kingdom isn't that we may go to Heaven when we die, but that we are able to come into the very presence of the living God now, while we are alive on earth.

The good news is that, as a consequence of what Jesus achieved in giving His own spotless life in place of ours, we are able to inherit eternal life now, whilst we are on earth.

Jesus proved that He had overcome sin and death on our behalf, by rising again from the dead.

On our own merit, there is nothing that we can do to earn or work our way into God's kingdom.

It is only when we realise that and accept what Jesus has done for us that we are able to begin to see how lost and failed we are.

When we realise our lost situation we can see that our only hope is in Jesus.

It is not until we understand that we are lost sinners with no hope, that we are in a position to come to Jesus, apologise for the way that we are and ask Him for forgiveness; a gift which He will willingly pour over us - it is the reason He came to earth.

We have been living, without realising it, in a kingdom of darkness; a kingdom of sin and ultimately, death - that is satan's kingdom.

When we appreciate this and ask, Jesus is keen to welcome us into God's kingdom of life.

Then we are able to cross over from one kingdom into another; from death into life - from satan's kingdom into God's kingdom.

There is no way that we are able to enter God's kingdom other than through Jesus - He is the door, the gate, the place of access.

We can look back at the conversation that Jesus had with His disciples shortly before He was crucified.

Jesus told them that He was going back to His Father.

Thomas asked Jesus the way to the Father:

Jesus told him, "I am the way, the truth, and the life. No one can come to the Father except through me.
John 14:6.

Entry into God's kingdom is through Jesus.

We talked earlier about a man called Nicodemus who came to Jesus at night. He was enquiring about God's kingdom and Jesus told him:

Jesus replied, "I assure you, no one can enter the kingdom of God without being born of water and the Spirit.

Humans can reproduce only human life, but the Holy Spirit gives birth to spiritual life.
John 3:5-6.

Incidentally, this is one of the sixty six times that Jesus used the phrase, *"I solemnly tell you"*, that we talked about when He was talking to the thief on the cross, *"I tell you today"*, or, *"verily, verily, I say unto you"*.

Our translators have given us here, *"I assure you"*.

It is the way that Jesus began a statement that was to be taken notice of.

We can be sure that Nicodemus took notice, and we should too.

Jesus told Nicodemus that no one is able to enter God's kingdom except through water (baptism) and the Spirit (the indwelling of God's Spirit within us).

It is not until we take a step of faith in showing that we trust in the salvation of Jesus, by being baptised in water, that God's Spirit will come and make His home with us.

We will be born again into God's family within a new kingdom.

If there is no indication in a person that God's Spirit is with them, we might wonder if they have truly placed their trust in Jesus.

Paul experienced this very problem:

Paul came across some believers who had not received God's Spirit and, after some questioning, understood the problem immediately and put the matter right.

While Apollos was in Corinth, Paul travelled through the interior regions until he reached Ephesus, on the coast, where he found several believers.

"Did you receive the Holy Spirit when you believed?" he asked them.

"No," they replied, "we haven't even heard that there is a Holy Spirit."

"Then what baptism did you experience?" he asked. And they replied, "The baptism of John."

Paul said, "John's baptism called for repentance from sin. But John himself told the people to believe in the one who would come later, meaning Jesus."

As soon as they heard this, they were baptised in the name of the Lord Jesus.

Then when Paul laid his hands on them, the Holy Spirit came on them, and they spoke in other tongues and prophesied.
Acts of the Apostles 19:1-6.

This group were followers of John the Baptist, who had been beheaded.

John had told them about Jesus.

The problem for them was that they hadn't entered into God's kingdom and received the Spirit of God, because they hadn't known the full truth of what Jesus had achieved for them.

Unless we appreciate our position and also what Jesus has done - what He accomplished, we have nothing to base our faith on and it is by faith that we are saved, not by our actions or words.

For it is by grace you have been saved, through faith - and this is not from yourselves, it is the gift of God.
Ephesians 2:8 NIV

There are many who might make an emotional remark or signal that they want to come into God's kingdom without any true understanding or appreciation of their situation.

They may go through a process of baptism but perhaps there is no real faith.

Many have gone through the process but without the faith that is necessary, there can be no salvation.

This will be evident by their unchanged lifestyle - by the fact that God's Spirit is not with them.

There are some who are taught that by taking communion they can receive eternal life.

There are others who are told that by passing certain theological exercises or a series of church courses they will receive eternal life.

There are many who may have been baptised in water, but without faith in the saving power of Jesus, they will not have entered God's kingdom.

Faith is a tangible substance and is an essential ingredient in our new birth.

God knows who are His and will only make His home with those He knows.

When the disciples received the gift of God's Spirit at Pentecost, they were overpowered by the presence of God - the people around thought that they were drunk.

At that time Peter stood up to explain to those around what was happening.

At the end of this explanation about Jesus and the events that had gone before, he said:

"So let everyone in Israel know for certain that God has made this Jesus, whom you crucified, to be both Lord and Messiah!"

Peter's words pierced their hearts, and they said to him and to the other apostles, "Brothers, what should we do?"

Peter replied, "Each of you must repent of your sins and turn to God, and be baptised in the name of Jesus Christ for the forgiveness of your sins.

Then you will receive the gift of the Holy Spirit.
This promise is to you, to your children, and to those far away - all who have been called by the Lord our God."
Acts of the Apostles 2:36-39.

Peter was repeating what Jesus had told Nicodemus.

Once we have realised our situation and repented, we are able to take a step of faith in the fact that Jesus has saved us from the threat of an eternal death and a life that is full of sin, and we can be baptised in water.

The Holy Spirit will then become one with us - the gift of the Spirit.

Many people refer to the gift of the Spirit as being baptised in the Spirit - such is the overwhelming presence of God in our new lives.

There is much to be said about being baptised in water and those who want to make this step of faith will need to be taught the incredible power that is involved, but this is not the place.

I have given much information on this, and other important subjects, in my book, Our Foundations, but today's subject is God's kingdom.

God's Spirit.

We might ask, why do we need God's Spirit?

The easy answer to that question is that we can do nothing purposeful, worthwhile, or that will last, without having God involved.

God is Spirit.

In order to become one with God, we too must become Spirit.

Unless we become one with God in receiving His Spirit we will remain unchanged.

God's kingdom is an everlasting kingdom.

There are two aspects to moving into and building God's kingdom.

One has to do with the kingdom of death, that we have left, and the other has to do with our new life.

When we enter God's kingdom we become a new creation - a Spiritual being.

This is as a consequence of our becoming one with God.

We cannot become one with God unless He becomes one with us - Spirit baptism.

Paul wrote to the Corinthian followers about this:

Therefore, if anyone is in Christ, the new creation has come: The old has gone, the new is here!
2 Corinthians 5:17 NIV

With that change comes a new way of thinking and living. - our minds will be restored; renewed.

In the old kingdom that we have left, our mind was imperfect, to say the least; our thoughts, and consequently our words and actions, were flawed because the enemy had planted corruption in our old lives.

God's Spirit will renew our thoughts to bring them in line with truth - God's thoughts.

"My thoughts are nothing like your thoughts," says the Lord. "And my ways are far beyond anything you could imagine.
Isaiah 55:8.

In this way we are able to be released from the power that the enemy had of ordering our life.

We are freed from the thoughts that previously persuaded us to say or do things that are harmful.

Because God's Spirit is speaking to us; guiding us, we are able to make sensible, fruitful decisions instead.

Entering into God's kingdom is an entrance into a new life.

We will be continually growing, changing, adapting and learning.

We are being changed to take on the likeness of Jesus.

Paul put it in this way:

But whenever someone turns to the Lord, the veil is taken away.
For the Lord is the Spirit, and wherever the Spirit of the Lord is, there is freedom.

So all of us who have had that veil removed can see and reflect the glory of the Lord.
And the Lord - who is the Spirit - makes us more and more like him as we are changed into his glorious image.
2 Corinthians 3:16-18.

If we are not being changed in this way we might want to retrace our steps to discover why.

The missing ingredient is often faith, but there can be other reasons, such as disobedience or a lack of understanding.

We are being changed to reflect Jesus.

God is love, therefore if we are one with Him our lives will also reflect that love, as we are being changed.

I quote from Paul's letters frequently, mainly because we have an ample supply of them, in comparison to the few that remain of the other disciples, in our Bibles.

Paul had a good grasp of living in the kingdom and we can benefit from his teaching with regards to the obstacles that the enemy might put in our way.

Paul wrote to the Corinthian followers about how they should learn to live in a loving manner.

If we want to enter and enjoy all that God's kingdom is, we too need to explore his advice and prayerfully take on God's character - which is selfless love.

The purpose being that the world can see Jesus appearing among us.

I pray that they will all be one, just as you and I are one - as you are in me, Father, and I am in you. And may they be in us so that the world will believe you sent me.
John 17:21.

What Jesus achieved for us is amazing.

How the Spirit enables us to change into His likeness is also continual and amazing.

But the reason is not ultimately for our own benefit - although we can be eternally grateful and rejoice in His selfless gift, and wonder as we are changed into His glorious likeness; the reason for our change in reflecting Jesus in our united life together is, *'so that the world might believe'*.

How will the world believe?

The main thrust of Jesus' conversation with His disciples at His last Passover meal, before He was crucified, was to do with our becoming one with each other, with Him and with the Father - a unity in thought and deed. *John 14.*

The prayer that Jesus prayed in the garden of Gethsemane before He was taken away was also about His followers becoming one:

"I am praying not only for these disciples but also for all who will ever believe in me through their message.

I pray that they will all be one, just as you and I are one - as you are in me, Father, and I am in you. And may they be in us so that the world will believe you sent me. John 17:20-21.

In order to discover whether Jesus' prayers are being answered, let us truthfully reply to some questions:

Do we live as one with each other?

The kingdom of God is not built upon church services, church attendance or theological qualifications.

God is not so much interested in our weekly church attendance, no matter how charismatic they are, how well rehearsed the praise team might be, or how gifted the pastor is.

He is looking for those who are obedient.

His kingdom is built upon relationships and not on church attendance or membership.

God's kingdom is built upon true relationships that are sealed in love.

Do we minister in love to each other?

Do we carry the burdens of others?

Do we share our lives?

Many of us attend church services, possibly chat and go home to wait until the next church service.

Does this way of life reflect the love of Jesus in our lives and relationships to the world?

Is the kingdom of God being manifested to the world through our loving lifestyles and bonding with each other?

Do we talk about others behind their backs?

This kind of talk creates division and disharmony.

Those who do this can not enter God's kingdom.

The Lord prayed for our unity.

Is our unity with others reflected in the cliques that we meet with?

Are we open with whom we fellowship?

Do we reach out to include others?

Do our many denominational divides reflect a unity to the world?

Putting our lack of unity to one side, do our individual lives reflect the love of Jesus?

When we are tired and irritable, do we consider others?

When we come across an obstacle do we place our trust in the Lord?

Do we cling on to fears or phobias?

Are we subject to habits and addictions?

Do we hold on to unforgiveness?

Are there people we don't talk to?

Are our children well mannered and obedient?

Do we love those who are difficult to get on with?

Do we truly live righteous lives?

Is there immorality amongst the members of the body of Christ?

When we truthfully answer these questions, and some that I haven't listed that we know about, we can clearly see that we have a lot of dismantling of division, and a very long way to go in our own growth and maturity, before we can say that the kingdom of God is being reflected to the world.

Jesus' prayer was *'that the world might believe'*.

The church structure and face as it is traditionally revealed to the world, has and is, doing much to turn those who need Jesus, away.

The responsibility for this situation being changed, lies in our own hands.

We need to come out of the structures that are a part of the Babylon that will be pulled down, and begin to build true, loving relationships that are born out of Spirit, with each other, apart from the doctrines and rituals of man.

Then I heard another voice calling from Heaven, "Come away from her, my people. Do not take part in her sins, or you will be punished with her.
Revelation 18:4.

The dark age of church is passing.

The age of God's kingdom is upon us.

We will not enjoy the new wine if we remain within the old wine skin.

If we want to experience the return of Jesus, these are some of the issues that, together, we must face and overcome.

It is as we learn to overcome these problems that the kingdom of God will begin to be manifested on earth and to be seen by the world - and then the world will believe.

The truth is that we will be unable to overcome these issues alone, but it will require a new type of relationship with others to be built.

There is a built in dependency upon others within God's kingdom.

Pulling down strongholds.

I mentioned that there are two aspects to entering and building God's kingdom on earth.

Our changed character and lifestyle leading into a useful unity of people who reflect the character of Jesus to the world is one aspect.

The other aspect is in reclaiming the ground that the enemy has taken.

Jesus defeated the enemy, who is satan, when He overcame death and sin on the cross.

We war against a defeated foe.

However, there are still battles to be won as he is evicted from the land that will become God's kingdom.

We have already talked about some of those areas that are yet to be reclaimed, but we may not be aware that they are strongholds of the enemy, or that they are yet to be overcome.

We are the ones whose job it is to overcome the enemy - to pull down strongholds and to be victorious.

In truth, the two aspects are a part of the same responsibility that we have in building God's kingdom.

The enemy has deceived us into believing that we are unable to change; that our characters will never be any different; that we will always have addictions and annoying habits, immaturity and that there can be no unity between us.

Those strongholds, that are in our mind, need to be demolished.

We need to have our minds renewed by the Spirit, who is one with us, in order to think God's thoughts - to understand the truth.

The truth is that we have been born into God's kingdom to be overcomers - to be victorious.

Until we appreciate and begin to live in that truth, the enemy will retain his grip on the life that has been given to us - we will not receive the life that is rightfully ours and we will not enter the kingdom that we have been offered.

Understanding these facts places some perspective on our life.

Paul wrote to the Corinthian Christians about these things:

Don't you realise that those who do wrong will not inherit the kingdom of God?

Don't fool yourselves.

Those who indulge in sexual sin, or who worship idols, or commit adultery, or are male prostitutes, or practice homosexuality, or are thieves, or greedy people, or drunkards, or are abusive, or cheat people - none of these will inherit the kingdom of God.
1 Corinthians 6:9-10.

"Ah", you might say, "but I'm not like those people".

Don't be so sure. Look again.

Paul may have been exaggerating the depths of their depravity but he was writing to people who had entered God's kingdom.

The people he was describing were no different from you and I.

Paul began his sentence by saying that, *'those who do wrong will not inherit God's kingdom'.*

Let's be honest about ourselves.

Do we do wrong?

The people that Paul was describing were not overcoming the enemy.

They had been deceived into believing they could never change, they were still living under the lies of satan who had told them they couldn't enjoy the good of God's kingdom; that they were failures and always would be; they were stuck with their addictions and habits and compulsive behaviours.

What kept them from enjoying God's kingdom was the fact that they believed Satan's lie that they could not change.

Are we so different?

Are we among those who do wrong?

Do we understand our responsibility; our purpose, living in God's kingdom?

Have we truly entered God's kingdom if we also believe those lies and do nothing about it?

The truth is, if we have the Spirit of God with us - we are a victorious people - if, and when, we respond.

Living in God's kingdom is about using the gifts that the Spirit has given us to overcome the enemy, in union with Father.

It is the enemy who keeps us from joining in fellowship with others.

We can overcome that when we work with Father.

This may include leaving our buildings to meet each other in a different way; perhaps in ones and twos in order to build strong relationships.

Do we need to restore relationships with our neighbours?

We are able to do that when we humble ourselves.

We can overcome habits and addictions when we hear the Spirit of God.

We can walk into healthy lifestyles when we follow the instructions He gives us.

We can dispose of fears and phobias when we learn to have faith in God instead.

We can claim freedom for the blind and cause the lame to walk when we are obedient to His voice.

You can ask for anything in my name, and I will do it, so that the Son can bring glory to the Father.

Yes, ask me for anything in my name, and I will do it!
"If you love me, obey my commandments.
John 14:13-15.

Living in God's kingdom is about proclaiming freedom for the captives - many of us are still captives.

The Spirit of the Sovereign Lord is upon me, for the Lord has anointed me to bring good news to the poor.

He has sent me to comfort the brokenhearted and to proclaim that captives will be released and prisoners will be freed.
Isaiah 61:1.

We will be able to bring good news to the poor and much more when we live in obedience to the rules governing His kingdom.

As we learn to live together in loving relationships, the Lord will introduce us to the gifts, tools and methods that are needed to bring down the strongholds that exist.

When the world can see us living in unity and in righteousness they will be seeing Jesus reflected in us; then they will also see the kingdom of God manifested on the earth.

We have been given tools and various giftings to enable us to pull down strongholds.

We must learn to recognise those and to use them.

Some might say that the enemy is already defeated; Jesus has defeated him.

When we look at our lives in reality we will see that there is some work to do.

Yes, the enemy is defeated but there is still ground that we need to take back - there are still those living in deception who believe they are helpless to do anything about their situation.

The enemy is defeated legally but practically he must be removed from the land if we are to own it and to live in it.

The Israelites had a similar problem.

Theirs was a physical battle; ours is a spiritual battle, but the principles are the same.

The Lord gave the promised land to the Israelites.

Legally it was theirs to live in.

But there were Canaanites living in the land that had to be destroyed or removed, before they could claim and enjoy it.

Ours is the same responsibility - the enemy is defeated, the land is ours, we must battle to take what is legally ours to enjoy.

We will find that as we learn to become one with Father and with each other; as we learn to demolish the strongholds that keep us, and others, in slavery to the whims of the enemy, the creation that we live in will also come under God's authority once more - to become fruitful and not under the curse that is destroying it at present.

We can understand why the enemy might want to distract us from that task by causing our minds to yearn to be taken away to Heaven, instead of us getting on with the business of taking the land that is rightfully ours.

He is a very skillful deceiver and has kept many of us in darkness about our mission and purpose for thousands of years.

The early church understood God's kingdom.

The Roman governments were so concerned about the growth of His kingdom that the early Christians were persecuted, martyred and scattered throughout the world.

They weren't looking to be swept away to Heaven but were convinced that Jesus' return was imminent.

And then the end will come.

There is a belief that we are close to becoming able to claim that the whole world has heard the gospel preached to them.

This target is based upon a misreading of the words that Jesus spoke to His disciples about the times that are to come.

And this gospel of the kingdom will be preached in the whole world as a testimony to all nations, and then the end will come.
Matthew 24:14 NIV.

Ironically, within the same conversation, Jesus also spoke about false teaching and heresies:

And many false prophets will appear and will deceive many people.
Matthew 24:11.

What has been preached throughout the world appears, on the face of it, to be a false gospel.

Paul referred to it as, a different gospel:

Let God's curse fall on anyone, including us or even an angel from Heaven, who preaches a different kind of Good News than the one we preached to you.

Galatians 1:8.

In reality there are few who have heard the gospel of the kingdom of God as we now understand a little of it.

There is even less evidence of the kingdom being manifested on the earth - as a testimony to all nations.

When the kingdom of God becomes a testimony to all nations then the end will come.

Let us begin building in order to speed the return of Jesus.

There is much for us to work on.

Jesus' return.

When the Bride of Christ - those of us who are obedient and are known by Jesus, has adorned herself with robes of righteousness, Jesus, who is the Groom, will return for His Bride.

Let us be glad and rejoice, and let us give honour to him. For the time has come for the wedding feast of the Lamb, and his bride has prepared herself.

She has been given the finest of pure white linen to wear." For the fine linen represents the good deeds of God's holy people.
Revelation 19:7-8.

Those who know him will be restored from the dead and those who know him and are still alive, will be united.

The ones who choose not to enter His kingdom while they are alive will stay in their graves until a later time when their decisions will be judged.

Will we be restored at that time and recognised as belonging to the Bride of Christ?

It is a serious question that we need to ask ourselves.

In the book of Revelation, John is given letters to write to various churches with regards to their need for change, in order to become pleasing to God.

There are warnings for those who do not listen to that voice and a promise of rewards that will be given to those who do listen and respond.

Within those warnings Jesus is calling us to change the way we are living, battle the enemy and to become overcomers.

We are called conquerors for a reason.

No, despite all these things, overwhelming victory is ours through Christ, who loved us.
Romans 8:37.

Paul wrote about us being conquerors because there is an enemy to defeat.

Paul is convinced that we are able to overcome him too.

He wasn't waiting around to be transported to Heaven but battling and overcoming the enemy daily - reclaiming God's kingdom on earth.

Those who enter the battle, and overcome, will receive the rewards of a conqueror when Jesus returns, those who don't will be judged accordingly.

One of those rewards is that we will reign with Him.

Paul wrote to Timothy about this:

If we endure hardship, we will reign with him. If we deny him, he will deny us.
2 Timothy 2:12.

Jesus told John to write about the rewards that are in store for those who are victorious:

Those who are victorious will sit with me on my throne, just as I was victorious and sat with my Father on his throne.
Revelation 3:21.

John saw the rewards of those who had their minds renewed - those who had become obedient and victorious over the enemy.

Then I saw thrones, and the people sitting on them had been given the authority to judge.

And I saw the souls of those who had been beheaded for their testimony about Jesus and for proclaiming the word of God.

They had not worshipped the beast or his statue, nor accepted his mark on their foreheads or their hands.

They all came to life again, and they reigned with Christ for a thousand years.

This is the first resurrection. (The rest of the dead did not come back to life until the thousand years had ended.)

Blessed and holy are those who share in the first resurrection.

For them the second death holds no power, but they will be priests of God and of Christ and will reign with him a thousand years.
Revelation 20:4-6.

Those who had been beheaded may be martyrs, but martyrs were killed in many other ways other than beheading.

The reference to beheading is more likely to be referring to those who have had their minds renewed.

Their heads, full of deception, have been "cut off" to be replaced by the mind of Christ'. *(extract from the commentary on the book of Revelation by J. J. Sweetman. Reproduced by permission).*

The extent to which we overcome in battles during this life on earth, will be reflected in the responsibilities that we are given in the kingdom when Jesus returns.

Jesus gave many examples of this principle in His teaching, with parables:

He replied, "You are permitted to understand the secrets of the kingdom of Heaven, but others are not.

To those who listen to my teaching, more understanding will be given, and they will have an abundance of knowledge.

But for those who are not listening, even what little understanding they have will be taken away from them.

That is why I use these parables, For they look, but they don't really see. They hear, but they don't really listen or understand.
Matthew 13:11-13.

And also:

To those who use well what they are given, even more will be given, and they will have an abundance.

But from those who do nothing, even what little they have will be taken away.

Now throw this useless servant into outer darkness, where there will be weeping and gnashing of teeth.'
Matthew 25:29-30.

There are   seven specific rewards in the book of Revelation that will be given to those who battle and overcome:

The word in the scripture that we have for overcome comes from a Greek word - *'nikh'*.

Sports fans might recognise that it is related to the word, *nike.*

The Bible is littered with references to our ability to overcome.

The scriptures relating to overcomers, or conquerors, are almost invariably linked with references to the rewards that overcomers will receive when Jesus appears on the earth.

The gift of a responsibility to reign with Jesus in His kingdom, is dependent upon our ability to overcome now.

Here are some others:

The first reward that is spoken of in the book of Revelation is that of having the fruit of the tree of life:

"Anyone with ears to hear must listen to the Spirit and understand what he is saying to the churches. To everyone who is victorious I will give fruit from the tree of life in the paradise of God.

Revelation 2:7.

We first hear about the tree of life in the book of Genesis where it has a place in the garden.

We find it again here in the book of Revelation, in the eternity of God.

There are also references to the tree of life in the psalms.

It is the tree that is the source of eternal life, but that is only a part of it.

It is a tree that brings fruitfulness, abundance, and life in all of its fullness.

The tree is Jesus, who is the source of life itself.

Are we overcoming?

In truth, Jesus, who is life itself, will be given to those who are victorious.

The second reward is that those who are victorious won't be harmed by the second death.

"Anyone with ears to hear must listen to the Spirit and understand what he is saying to the churches.

Whoever is victorious will not be harmed by the second death.
Revelation 2:11.

Paul speaks about us crucifying our flesh.

Those who belong to Christ Jesus have nailed the passions and desires of their sinful nature to his cross and crucified them there.
Galatians 5:24.

Paul is talking about ridding ourselves of the self nature that comes between us and God.

One of the aims of the enemy is to entice us to focus on ourselves; our comfort, our security, our wellbeing, our status etc.

If we cling to those things we will inevitably be separated from Jesus.

When we overcome the enticements of the enemy we will rid ourselves of the distractions that cause us harm and Jesus will be able to rise up in our lives.

When we die to ourselves we will have no reason to fear the second death as we will be free of anything in it that may harm us.

We will look again at the second death later.

The third reward for overcomers is hidden manna and a white stone, with a new name.

"Anyone with ears to hear must listen to the Spirit and understand what he is saying to the churches.

To everyone who is victorious I will give some of the manna that has been hidden away in Heaven.

And I will give to each one a white stone, and on the stone will be engraved a new name that no one understands except the one who receives it.
Revelation 2:17.

'Manna', was how the Israelites described the food that God sent each day, apart from the sabbath, to feed them when they were in the wilderness.

The word means, what is it?

The Israelites hadn't seen or tasted anything like it before and therefore they called it, *what is it?*

The hidden manna in the book of Revelation describes the words of Jesus, that only those who are close to Him will hear and comprehend.

It is hidden in the sense that others have not known it and will not understand it.

Today we find that many scriptures that have been hidden to our understanding in previous times, are now being revealed to those who God can trust.

The hidden manna of God is food for the ones who need Heavenly sustenance in their lives.

Jesus referred to Himself as The bread of life:

Jesus replied, "I am the bread of life. Whoever comes to me will never be hungry again. Whoever believes in me will never be thirsty.
John 6:35.

A white stone is a reference to the way a court was held in Roman times.

A jury within the courts of the time produced a black stone when a person was judged guilty, and a white stone when they were judged as innocent.

We are judged innocent, not because of anything we have achieved, but because we have been bought out of a state of sin through the sacrifice of Jesus.

On the white stone will be a new name which will be an indication of the trials and victories we have encountered.

It will describe our character and will only be known by ourselves and the Lord.

We have partially covered the next reward already:

*To all who are victorious, who obey me to the very end,
To them I will give authority over all the nations.*

*They will rule the nations with an iron rod and smash
them like clay pots.*

*They will have the same authority I received from my
Father, and I will also give them the morning star!*

*"Anyone with ears to hear must listen to the Spirit and
understand what he is saying to the churches.
Revelation 2:26-29.*

There appears to be a harshness within The New Living
translation of the Bible.

But Jesus is talking about the same thing that He told
His disciples, and us, to pray towards:

*'May your kingdom come, may your will be done on
earth, as it is in Heaven'. (Matt. 6:10.)*

In other translations the word *'sceptre'* has been used
instead of rod.

The rod is another word for sceptre and originates in the
idea that a ruler of a nation is a person who shepherds
his people, or guides them.

We can see from the verse that the sceptre of the Lord, which is a sign of authority, has been given to the ones who overcome.

The nations will look to those in authority for guidance as Jesus reigns.

The phrase that the, *'nations will be smashed like clay pots'*, is a reference to the fact that there is, and will further be, a need for the clay pots which represent our self nature to be smashed apart, to be replaced by God's nature; God's character of love.

There is an indication here of the fact that we are reigning with Jesus on the earth - Jesus has become reflected in us as one person and that many from all nations will be coming to the Lord as a consequence of that reflection.

Overcomers will also receive The Morning Star.

Peter relates The Morning Star to words of prophecy:

Because of that experience, we have even greater confidence in the message proclaimed by the prophets.

You must pay close attention to what they wrote, for their words are like a lamp shining in a dark place - until the Day dawns, and Christ the Morning Star shines in your hearts.
2 Peter 1:19.

Jesus told John that He is The Morning Star.

"I, Jesus, have sent my angel to give you this message for the churches.

I am both the source of David and the heir to his throne. I am the bright morning star."
Revelation 22:16.

Those who overcome will receive Jesus; the spirit of prophecy, who is The Morning Star.

Another reward that those who overcome will receive is purity - righteousness, the promise that our names will never be removed from the book of life and adoption into Jesus.

All who are victorious will be clothed in white.

I will never erase their names from the Book of Life, but I will announce before my Father and his angels that they are mine.

"Anyone with ears to hear must listen to the Spirit and understand what he is saying to the churches.
Revelation 3:5-6.

All who are victorious will be clothed in white.

White robes speak about righteousness.

Our righteousness has to do with obedience; the manner in which we respond to the prompting of the Spirit.

Abraham was a man who is accounted as being righteous because he believed God.

And Abram believed the Lord, and the Lord counted him as righteous because of his faith.
Genesis 15:6.

When we place our trust in God we activate a thing called faith.

It is faith in God that is the engine that is creative in our lives.

It is not our abilities (works) that count as righteousness but what Father is able to achieve as a consequence of our faith in Him; our response to His prompting.

We are to be clothed in the righteousness of Jesus, which are the things that we do in faith.

I doubt if this refers to the fact that we will literally wear white clothing - but it might.

The righteousness of God refers to the whole being of the one who has been redeemed from sin and death.

We can link this with the vision of an event that John was shown in Heaven:

Let us rejoice and be glad and give him glory! For the wedding of the Lamb has come, and his bride has made herself ready.

Fine linen, bright and clean, was given to her to wear."
(Fine linen stands for the righteous acts of God's holy people.)
Revelation 19:8 NIV

Our names will never be removed from the book of life.

The book of life is the place where everyone's name is written before that name is blotted out as a consequence of sin.

The Lord replied to Moses, "Whoever has sinned against me I will blot out of my book.
Exodus 32:33 NIV

If we want our name to be written back in that book we need to become overcomers.

We can only be overcomers if we know Jesus and listen and respond to His voice.

Entering God's kingdom is not a case of a one off response to a call from an evangelist, but a continual responsive nature during our lives.

When our names are written in the book of life Jesus will represent us in the courts of Heaven and will claim us as His own before His Father.

There are four further rewards for those who overcome within the next promises:

"Because you have obeyed my command to persevere, I will protect you from the great time of testing that will come upon the whole world to test those who belong to this world.

I am coming soon. Hold on to what you have, so that no one will take away your crown.

All who are victorious will become pillars in the Temple of my God, and they will never have to leave it.

And I will write on them the name of my God, and they will be citizens in the city of my God - the New Jerusalem that comes down from Heaven from my God.

And I will also write on them my new name.

"Anyone with ears to hear must listen to the Spirit and understand what he is saying to the churches.
Revelation 3:10-13.

From the sixth of the letters that John was told to write to the followers of Jesus, we have a promise that we will be protected from a time of testing, that is to come upon those who belong to the world.

Some have referred to this time of testing as a period of tribulation that is to come.

Jesus told His disciples that they would have troubles:

I have told you all this so that you may have peace in me. Here on earth you will have many trials and sorrows.

But take heart, because I have overcome the world."
John 16:33.

James referred to it in this way:

Dear brothers and sisters, when troubles of any kind come your way, consider it an opportunity for great joy.

For you know that when your faith is tested, your endurance has a chance to grow.

So let it grow, for when your endurance is fully developed, you will be perfect and complete, needing nothing.
James 1:2-4.

Jesus has said that He will protect us from these times of troubles and to *fear not,* because He has overcome the world.

We can safely assume then that the fear and panic that some preachers attempt to instil in their congregations when talking about a great tribulation, can be ignored.

There will be times of trials and troubles but we can rejoice when we come across these as we will be protected and they are only there in order to test our faith and to build our endurance.

Yes, there will come increasing times of difficulty.

These times will come in order to prompt those who don't know Him to seek Him out while there is still time to do so.

We can see these times and events occurring now and becoming more regular and intense, but for us who know Him, and are learning to become overcomers, we have a built in protection from the Lord whilst we abide in Him.

Jesus encourages us to *'hold on to what we have'*.

The enemy seeks to devour us and take away the rewards that we have won.

We need to be increasingly vigilant and to hold on to that.

Overcomers will be *'pillars in the temple of God, and they will never leave it'*.

A pillar speaks of strength and support.

Jesus is referring to the people of God as His temple; it is the place where He dwells in permanence..

Overcomers will be the strength and support of the people of God and they will never leave His presence.

We will be, and already are, citizens of the New Jerusalem.

The New Jerusalem is descriptive of the situation that will be when Heaven comes to earth.

The New Jerusalem is even now descending as we take our place within God's kingdom.

This is not, as some suggest, a future event but an ongoing event that is appearing as God's kingdom is established on earth.

We are not going to Heaven one day, but, as we take our place; become overcomers and establish His kingdom on earth - Heaven - the New Jerusalem, is coming to earth.

We are given a new name.

In naming a thing or person, ownership is claimed.

Our new name indicates that we are owned by God and belong to Him and are with Him.

There are many rewards for those who listen to His voice and become overcomers, let's hear about some more:

"Look! I stand at the door and knock. If you hear my voice and open the door, I will come in, and we will share a meal together as friends.

Those who are victorious will sit with me on my throne, just as I was victorious and sat with my Father on his throne.

"Anyone with ears to hear must listen to the Spirit and understand what he is saying to the churches."
Revelation 3:22.

The seventh letter that John was asked to write was addressed to the Christians at Laodicea.

The Laodiceans represent people who are lukewarm.

They are people who don't really care but they will turn up when required, just to show willing.

They are those who have followed the rituals, but missed out on the life changing event of being truly born again, they are not concerned about whether the kingdom gets built or not.

They believe that their place is secured and nothing more needs to be done.

Perhaps they are those who are waiting to go to Heaven or for the rapture.

Jesus warns them what will happen unless they embrace change; He will *'spit them out of His mouth'*

They are people who leave a nasty taste - an unpleasant flavour.

But even to these people Jesus urges that, if they would only begin to start listening to Him and open the door, He will be delighted to come and enjoy a meal with them.

Even these people might still be given a place in His kingdom, to reign with Him, if they listen and open the door to Him.

Even those who have very little faith and do not achieve very much can be given a place to reign - God can do much with very little.

But when we consider how much the Lord did on our behalf, why wouldn't we also want to go above and beyond the place of just escaping from the flames!

For no one can lay any foundation other than the one we Anyone who builds on that foundation may use a variety of materials - gold, silver, jewels, wood, hay, or straw.

But on the judgement day, fire will reveal what kind of work each builder has done. The fire will show if a person's work has any value.

If the work survives, that builder will receive a reward. But if the work is burned up, the builder will suffer great loss.

The builder will be saved, but like someone barely escaping through a wall of flames.
1 Corinthians 3:11-15.

Notice the insistence after each letter in the book of Revelation, that, *"Anyone with ears to hear must listen to the Spirit and understand what he is saying to the churches.*

We might want to take some time to look into these scriptures to enquire as to why The Lord was so insistent and whether we might need to take steps to put some things in order.

At the start of this chapter we were prompted to ask the question:

Will we be restored at that time and recognised as belonging to the Bride of Christ?

We were brought into God's kingdom in order to be overcomer's - to be victorious over the enemy - to live in God's abundant life.

If we find we are struggling to get by; under pressure to get through the day, we might want to find out why that is.

The Spirit doesn't give birth to defeat.

The Israelites experienced defeat at Ai, after they had captured Jericho.

They found there were good reasons for their difficulties.

Their answers were discovered by asking the Lord - *Joshua 7*.

We do not live in the way of defeat. If we do, we must discover why.

The Spirit is always ready to point us in the right direction.

Take a look at Joshua chapter seven and listen to what the Spirit is saying.

The millennial reign of Jesus.

Blessed and holy are those who share in the first resurrection. For them the second death holds no power, but they will be priests of God and of Christ and will reign with him a thousand years.
Revelation 20:6.

Blessed are those who wash their robes.

They will be permitted to enter through the gates of the city and eat the fruit from the tree of life.

Outside the city are the dogs - the sorcerers, the sexually immoral, the murderers, the idol worshipers, and all who love to live a lie.
Revelation 22:14‑15.

The world cannot and will not enter the city of God; the New Jerusalem, which is His body.

Outside the city are the dogs:

The Greek word that we have here as dogs is linked with sorcerers.

It is often alternatively interpreted as hypocrites.

They are the ones who are deceived - sorcery is deception - they are people who live in a world of lies.

These are the same people as the ones who are not overcomers that Paul spoke about.

These are the ones who had the opportunity to rid themselves of deception but didn't take it.

These are the ones who chose to wait and see.

Paul wrote to the Corinthians:

Don't you realise that those who do wrong will not inherit the kingdom of God?

Jesus also called the people who cried out, "Lord, Lord", 'those who do wrong', so we are not talking about the dregs of the earth, but often people who appear to be quite nice.

"Not everyone who calls out to me, 'Lord! Lord!' will enter the kingdom of Heaven. Only those who actually do the will of my Father in Heaven will enter.

On judgement day many will say to me, 'Lord! Lord! We prophesied in your name and cast out demons in your name and performed many miracles in your name.'

But I will reply, 'I never knew you. Get away from me, you who break God's laws.'
Matthew 7:21-23.

Paul went on to write:

Don't fool yourselves. Those who indulge in sexual sin, or who worship idols, or commit adultery, or are male prostitutes, or practice homosexuality, or are thieves, or greedy people, or drunkards, or are abusive, or cheat people - none of these will inherit the kingdom of God. 1 Corinthians 6:9-10.

We might ask ourselves the question, have we taken the opportunity to tackle the deceptions and shortcomings in our own lives?

Have we listened to and responded to the truth that comes from the voice of God, or pleased ourselves?

Do we minister to others in order to bring freedom to them also?

Will we be included in the number that are the Bride of Christ?

In truth Jesus is appearing on earth now and has been returning since He went back to His Father.

The process of His return has been delayed by the lack of understanding of our responsibility in bringing about that return.

The Lord has been patient with us.

When we actively begin to live in the truth of His word He will be reflected in us; Jesus will be seen on earth through His body.

Then news of His kingdom will be preached on earth and the nations of the world will hear it:

And the Good News about the kingdom will be preached throughout the whole world, so that all nations will hear it; and then the end will come.
Matthew 24:14.

The end that Jesus referred to is not the end of the world; far from it.

Paul wrote to the Roman followers about the fact that the whole of creation is waiting to be released from the slavery that it endures now:

The creation looks forward to the day when it will join God's children in glorious freedom from death and decay.

For we know that all creation has been groaning as in the pains of childbirth right up to the present time.
Romans 8:21-22.

We too can be assured that the creation is being, and will be, restored, despite the apparent events that would suggest the contrary.

The events that we see occurring now; the turmoil and upheavals; world wide disasters and also localised catastrophe's are for the world to appreciate that the Lord reigns.

They are also for the body of Christ to realise that it is time to grow up into a place of maturity and to live in the responsibility that we have been given.

Time is running out.

It is for the world and us, to seize these last hours that we have as an opportunity for reconciliation.

The end that Jesus referred to was the end of the deception of satan.

When Jesus returns it will be satan's end that will come.

Then there will be a period of restoration on earth.

The scripture gives us a period of one thousand years, during which satan will be bound.

Then I saw an angel coming down from Heaven with the key to the bottomless pit and a heavy chain in his hand. He seized the dragon - that old serpent, who is the devil, Satan - and bound him in chains for a thousand years.

The angel threw him into the bottomless pit, which he then shut and locked so Satan could not deceive the nations anymore until the thousand years were finished.

Afterward he must be released for a little while.
Revelation 20:1-3.

Whether this is a specific period of time or an unknown period is a subject of some debate.

There are some who suggest that satan was bound when Jesus overcame him in His death and resurrection, and he continues to be bound now.

Satan has no power to continue to enslave those who wish to be free of him and his influence.

In that sense, he is bound.

There is some truth in that statement and If that is the case then we are already living within that millennium period.

But our verse suggests that when this occurs he will be unable to deceive the nations and we know that now he does continue to deceive.

Jesus is clearly returning as we look to see Him reflected amongst His people.

We are beginning to learn to reign with Him on earth.

Whilst satan is bound Jesus will reign until the time comes for him to be released again.

During this period many millions will choose Jesus from around the globe.

There will be an immense ingathering of people; a harvest of people during that time.

Then I saw a white cloud, and seated on the cloud was someone like the Son of Man.
He had a gold crown on his head and a sharp sickle in his hand.

Then another angel came from the Temple and shouted to the one sitting on the cloud, "Swing the sickle, for the time of harvest has come; the crop on earth is ripe."

So the one sitting on the cloud swung his sickle over the earth, and the whole earth was harvested.

After that, another angel came from the Temple in Heaven, and he also had a sharp sickle.
Then another angel, who had power to destroy with fire, came from the altar.
He shouted to the angel with the sharp sickle, "Swing your sickle now to gather the clusters of grapes from the vines of the earth, for they are ripe for judgement."

So the angel swung his sickle over the earth and loaded the grapes into the great winepress of God's wrath.

The grapes were trampled in the winepress outside the city, and blood flowed from the winepress in a stream about 180 miles long and as high as a horse's bridle. Revelation 14:14-20.

*John saw someone like the "Son of Man" sitting on a cloud, a name which Jesus often used to identify Himself with humanity.

But John was not entirely sure that who he saw was Jesus. Yet, the man had a gold crown which speaks of royalty. And John had heard an angel say that Jesus would return on a cloud (Acts 1).

In any event, elsewhere when John sees an angel, he is specific about what he sees.

The Son of Man held a sickle in his hand - a cutting instrument similar to a scythe, but with a longer and straighter blade and handle which allows a cleaner cut.

The scythe is used to destroy. Satan is often pictured with a scythe in his hands.

Another angel representing the Heavenly minded people of God, then came shouting that the harvest time had come.

This was the signal for the one like the Son of Man to swing his sickle and harvest the whole earth.

This was not a harvest of destruction. This was a harvest of those who were responding to the call of God.

When we read that the whole earth was harvested, it does not mean that everyone alive was brought into the kingdom of God.

Jesus taught that the weeds and good crops will grow together. And when the time of harvest comes there will be a separation between the good and evil.

After the first harvest another angel came for a second harvest. And then, yet another angel came with fire, which speaks of the word to purify the hearers.

It was a word of power. God is giving every opportunity for those on earth to respond to Him.

The angel with fire shouted to the angel with the sharp sickle to gather the grapes from the vines for they are ripe for judgement.

Grapes are the fruit of the vine. Jesus taught that He is the vine and we, His disciples, are the branches of the vine (John 15).

As the angel swung his sickle, it is our fruit which is harvested.

The Greek word translated as "wrath" can also mean "strong passion".

The truth is that God loves us with a strong passion. Therefore, instead of this passage meaning the judgement of God on the world, it means that God is harvesting the fruit of His saints He loves with a strong passion.

We need to always remember that this is a vision. And the events should not be taken literally.

For example, John saw blood flowing from the winepress in a stream about 180 miles long and as high as a horse's bridle. If taken literally the blood which flowed came from many times more than the population of the earth.

Other interpretations do not translate the Greek stadia into miles. Therefore, although the distance John saw could have been 180 or 140 miles, depending on the size of stadia, the important fact is that the distance was 1600 stadia.

The number 1600 is composed 40 times 40, or 4 x 4 x 10 x10.

Taking either way to compute the total, the number speaks of a time of great testing. The number 40 speaks of testing. And multiplied by itself speaks of total testing.

The number four speaks of the entirety. And the number 10 speaks of man's limitations.

Therefore, the time of testing is extreme, stretching our limitations to bear it.

The purpose of the testing is to refine us. God's ultimate intention is that we become the Bride of Christ.

That Bride will be those who have overcome the flesh; those who have overcome Satan. And for us to overcome, we need to be tested.

We are trampled outside the city. It is not God who is trampling us. It is persecution driven by Satan wanting to destroy any who have the life of God.
But it is allowed by God. He wants us to know even more blessings as we persevere under great hardship.

*(extract from a commentary on the book of Revelation by J. J. Sweetman).

The kingdom of God will be manifested on the earth.

When the times of the Gentiles are complete - that is the period that has been allotted for all of God's people to be redeemed, the doors will be shut and then the Israelite nation will see the kingdom of God and will be provoked to envy.

Did God's people stumble and fall beyond recovery?

Of course not! They were disobedient, so God made salvation available to the Gentiles.

But he wanted his own people to become jealous and claim it for themselves.

Now if the Gentiles were enriched because the people of Israel turned down God's offer of salvation, think how much greater a blessing the world will share when they finally accept it.
Romans 11:12.

It is then that many from the Israelite nation will understand and recognise Jesus as their Messiah.

They too will be grafted on again to the vine from where they were once removed.

Notice how God is both kind and severe.
He is severe toward those who disobeyed, but kind to you if you continue to trust in his kindness.

But if you stop trusting, you also will be cut off.
And if the people of Israel turn from their unbelief, they will be grafted in again, for God has the power to graft them back into the tree.

You, by nature, were a branch cut from a wild olive tree. So if God was willing to do something contrary to nature by grafting you into his cultivated tree, he will be far

more eager to graft the original branches back into the tree where they belong.
Romans 11:22-24.

When all have entered God's kingdom - the New Jerusalem, the enemy and deceiver of God's people will be released again.

At which time he will raise an army, in a last ditch attempt to destroy God's people.

It is inconceivable that there will be any unsaved people left who will flock to his side, given the manner in which Jesus implores all to come to Him in those last days.

But we are told that there will be a rebellious army who will not be refined by the fire of Jesus' love.

The scripture implies a large multitude that are arrayed against the children of God.

When we consider the demonic entities that rebelled and were thrown out of Heaven with satan I would expect these to be the army that is referred to.

They war against us on a daily basis individually, and the enemy will want them behind him at his last attempt to overthrow.

I believe that the army that is spoken of in the book of Revelation is a reference to the spiritual warfare that we encounter and battle against daily.

There may be a physical battle also but it is a spiritual war that we engage in.

For we are not fighting against flesh-and-blood enemies, but against evil rulers and authorities of the unseen world, against mighty powers in this dark world, and against evil spirits in the Heavenly places.
Ephesians 6:12.

The battle that the enemy will present to us is known as the battle of Armageddon.

It will be a last ditch onslaught on our minds by the demonic forces that wage war against us in an effort to entice any stragglers to fall away.

The word Armageddon is taken from the name of an ancient town which was known as *'Megiddo'*.

Armageddon means the mountain of *'Megiddo'*.

When scripture talks of mountains it is a reference to those who exalt themselves to high places; governments and authorities; people who do not live under the Lordship of Jesus and often the demonic entities that have strongholds in those places.

Megiddo was the site of many battles in the past because it was a site of strategic importance, being situated at a crossroads to and from various trade routes across the world.

Trade is also a reference to the finances that control much of the world's incentive and ambition.

The battle of Armageddon appears to occur after the fall of Babylon, which too is to do with the fall of all that holds itself high, in opposition to the rule of Jesus.

These would include governments, financial institutions, the counterfeit church and religious systems etc.

The enemy will be testing as to where our security lies.

What are we dependent upon, the love and security in the provision of the Lord? Or our wealth and position?

Perhaps this will be a time of greatest danger for those who have not battled against the enemy frequently.

They will not have gained experience or understanding of his deceitful ways.

They will still be living in their flesh.

We must ensure before it's too late that we become a well tuned army, able to pull down the strongholds that still exist in our lives.

We are called to battle on a daily basis; to have our minds renewed, for this very reason.

Soldiers need to practice warfare in readiness for the battle that must be won.

We wouldn't want to be the ones who had won much territory for it to be lost at the final battle.

The battle won't last very long and the enemy will be defeated.

When Jesus returns - When He is revealed to the nations, He will reign until every enemy is destroyed.

It is worth noting here that God's enemies are not nations or individuals but everything that raises itself up in opposition to Him.

For we are not fighting against flesh-and-blood enemies, but against evil rulers and authorities of the unseen world, against mighty powers in this dark world, and against evil spirits in the Heavenly places.
Ephesians 6:12.

For the Scriptures say, "God has put all things under his authority." (Of course, when it says "all things are under his authority," that does not include God himself, who gave Christ his authority.)

Then, when all things are under his authority, the Son will put himself under God's authority, so that God, who gave his Son authority over all things, will be utterly supreme over everything everywhere.
1 Corinthians 15:27-28.

'Your will be done on earth, as it is in Heaven', is an ongoing prayer that began in Jesus' time, as He proclaimed and initiated His kingdom, and will continue until all of His enemies are defeated.

After Armageddon - the second death.

We read about two deaths in scripture and two different resurrections of the dead.

The first death:

The first death is the death of ourselves, or *our flesh,* as Paul described it; that which is earthly and attached to the world:

My old self has been crucified with Christ. It is no longer I who live, but Christ lives in me. So I live in this earthly body by trusting in the Son of God, who loved me and gave himself for me.
Galatians 2:20.

And again in his letter to the Romans:

We know that our old sinful selves were crucified with Christ so that sin might lose its power in our lives. We are no longer slaves to sin.
For when we died with Christ we were set free from the power of sin.
Romans 6:6-7.

This first death is also linked with fire that the Lord uses to refine us through our trials:

As we learn to overcome the enemy, our flesh will be burned off in the fire of God's furnace - it is a refining fire.

"But who will be able to endure it when he comes? Who will be able to stand and face him when he appears? For he will be like a blazing fire that refines metal, or like a strong soap that bleaches clothes.
He will sit like a refiner of silver, burning away the dross.

He will purify the Levites, refining them like gold and silver, so that they may once again offer acceptable sacrifices to the Lord.
Malachi 3:2-3.

The prophet Malachi spoke about God burning off the dross in order to refine us.

He talked about the refining of the Levites, who were the priestly tribe from the nation of Israel.

The order of the priestly tribe of Levites has passed and we are now the priests who minister in God's temple:

He has made us a kingdom of priests for God his Father. All glory and power to him forever and ever! Amen.
Revelation 1:6.

John the baptist also preached about the fire that accompanies baptism for those who follow Jesus.

"I baptise with water those who repent of their sins and turn to God. But someone is coming soon who is greater than I am - so much greater that I'm not worthy even to be his slave and carry his sandals.

He will baptise you with the Holy Spirit and with fire.
Matthew 3:11.

Peter wrote about our trials being used to test and purify our faith, in the same way as fire is used to test and purify gold:

So be truly glad. There is wonderful joy ahead, even though you must endure many trials for a little while.

These trials will show that your faith is genuine. It is being tested as fire tests and purifies gold - though your faith is far more precious than mere gold.

So when your faith remains strong through many trials, it will bring you much praise and glory and honour on the day when Jesus Christ is revealed to the whole world.
1 Peter 1:6-.

Notice how Peter used the phrase of Jesus being *revealed to the world,* rather than Jesus returning to the world.

Paul talked about fire burning off that which is of no value in our lives, leaving behind that which is useful.

Anyone who builds on that foundation may use a variety of materials—gold, silver, jewels, wood, hay, or straw.

But on the judgement day, fire will reveal what kind of work each builder has done.

The fire will show if a person's work has any value.
1 Corinthians 3:12-13.

We can be sure that when scripture uses the word fire, it has to do with purification or refining.

God led the Israelite nation through the wilderness by fire at night.

He was in a cloud by day and a fire by night.

Both of these elements symbolised His presence.

The Lord went ahead of them. He guided them during the day with a pillar of cloud, and he provided light at night with a pillar of fire. This allowed them to travel by day or by night.
Exodus 13:21.

The Israelites were being refined as they followed the fire.

The Israelites were being transformed from having a slave mentality to that of being a free people, they were being trained to become a nation who were able to overcome the Canaanites.

From the experience that Moses had with the burning bush we can determine that God's fire is holy; it brings revelation; it brings clarity, but does not consume.

There the angel of the Lord appeared to him in a blazing fire from the middle of a bush. Moses stared in amazement.

Though the bush was engulfed in flames, it didn't burn up.
Exodus 3:2.

God's fire brings purity and righteousness.

Fire burns away all that is useless and not of any value, so that we are able to grow in Christ, to reach maturity.

If we die to ourselves by allowing God's fire to burn away that which is of no value, we need not fear the second death.

"Anyone with ears to hear must listen to the Spirit and understand what he is saying to the churches.

Whoever is victorious will not be harmed by the second death.
Revelation 2:11.

If we die once we will also reign with Jesus when He is revealed.

When Jesus is revealed, there will be a resurrection of those who were victorious during their lives.

They too will be raised to reign.

This is the first resurrection. (The rest of the dead did not come back to life until the thousand years had ended.)

Blessed and holy are those who share in the first resurrection. For them the second death holds no power, but they will be priests of God and of Christ and will reign with him a thousand years.
Revelation 20:5-6.

As we have discovered, at this time Jesus will reign with overcomers.

There will be a great battle as the deceiver attempts to drag some away from following the Lord, but the Lord encourages us to remain steadfast.

The Bible refers to this fight as Armageddon.

After a reign of one thousand years, when Jesus is fully revealed among His children, the enemy who is satan, will be defeated and thrown into a lake of fire, along with the beast and the false prophet.

The lake of fire is a symbolic phrase and not a reality.

The book of Revelation is not giving a picture of a physical future, but of how the Lord fights for us, and we must also fight the spiritual battles in our lives, to ensure that no one misses out on His love.

The lake of fire indicates an end of sin and unrighteousness.

The beast and the false prophet are both devious constructions of the enemy, who is satan.

The lake of fire indicates an end of all unrighteousness; an end of sin - all is burned up, leaving only righteousness.

When the bride of Christ grows to maturity, Jesus will be revealed in her and there will be no more unrighteousness forever.

The second resurrection and the second death.

In the visions that John had, he then saw something else:

I saw the dead, both great and small, standing before God's throne.

And the books were opened, including the Book of Life. And the dead were judged according to what they had done, as recorded in the books.

Then death and the grave were thrown into the lake of fire.
This lake of fire is the second death.

And anyone whose name was not found recorded in the Book of Life was thrown into the lake of fire.
Revelation 20:12-15.

We have discovered that those who are overcomers will not be harmed by the second death.

John saw all of those whose names are not written in the book of life, raised again to life.

This is the second resurrection.

These are the ones who Jesus referred to as those to whom He will say, *'I did not know you'*.

Clearly these people will be harmed by the second death.

We do not read that they will suffer for eternity.

We do not read that they will be condemned to hell for eternity.

Although hell is clearly where they have been living if they have not entered into God's kingdom.

Hell can be defined as living without God and, having experienced the life of many families and individuals who live without Jesus, I can understand how that term might apply.

Can we imagine a life filled with nothing of the life of Jesus; a world with no love?

Today everyone enjoys at least a small glimpse of the life, flowing from Jesus, that sustains the world that we live in.

There is some goodness, some joy, some pleasure, although limited.

I would not like to experience a life with none of these experiences.

But the lake of fire will end anything that is impure.

We might imagine that there will be weeping and gnashing of teeth, having missed the opportunity to welcome the free life of Jesus and all of those rewards:

And he will reply, 'I tell you, I don't know you or where you come from. Get away from me, all you who do evil.'

"There will be weeping and gnashing of teeth, for you will see Abraham, Isaac, Jacob, and all the prophets in the kingdom of God, but you will be thrown out.
Luke 13:27-28.

We are not given specific detail of what the lake of fire involves, for those who don't know Jesus.

We have seen that fire in scripture normally involves purification.

Paul issued some directions with regards to people who were spreading a false doctrine amongst the followers in Ephesus, to Timothy.

They were to be excluded from the presence of the believers until they had learnt not to blaspheme:

Cling to your faith in Christ, and keep your conscience clear. For some people have deliberately violated their consciences; as a result, their faith has been shipwrecked.

Hymenaeus and Alexander are two examples.

I threw them out and handed them over to Satan so they might learn not to blaspheme God.
1 Timothy 1:19‡20.

Paul handed Hymenaeus and Alexander over to Satan until they learnt not to blaspheme.

In practical terms this meant that they were excluded from the fellowship of the followers of Jesus until they learnt to listen and adhere to truth.

In the book of Revelation John is also shown a picture of New Jerusalem.

The New Jerusalem is a picture of the body of Christ - His children, who are overcomers.

It is a situation where evildoers; those who do wrong, are kept outside; they are not allowed to enter the gates.

They do not experience the life that emanates from Jesus in any way.

Blessed are those who wash their robes. They will be permitted to enter through the gates of the city and eat the fruit from the tree of life.

Outside the city are the dogs—the sorcerers, the sexually immoral, the murderers, the idol worshipers, and all who love to live a lie.
Revelation 22:14-15.

Those who wash their robes are permitted to enter through the gates.

It might appear to be apparent but it is probably worth mentioning that the New Jerusalem isn't a physical structure, but an illustration.

It is a picture of the body of Christ living in oneness with each other and with Jesus.

The walls aren't real walls, and the gates aren't real gates.

The gates illustrate the fact that there is no mixture inside of God's kingdom.

Those who do wrong, are still remaining outside of the gates when the New Jerusalem flows out of Heaven.

The fact that only the righteous are allowed within the walls of the city indicates that there are those who are unrighteous still outside, no doubt there will be some purification by fire to be finalised.

The good news is that there are gates in the walls of the city.

There is little gain to be made by offering speculation, but we might surmise that the lake of fire, that those who do wrong are thrown into, is a refining fire that will train even those who are entrenched in evil to a place of realisation and contrition.

There is no doubt that there will be much pain involved in that transition as realisation of their deception and loss is acquired.

We may also surmise that the lake of fire symbolises the situation today as those who are outside the body of Christ suffer the fire of refinement.

The New Jerusalem has gates that are firmly shut but the purpose of gates is to allow access as well as to bar - perhaps for the finally repentant.

The New Jerusalem.

I heard a loud shout from the throne, saying, "Look, God's home is now among his people! He will live with them, and they will be his people. God himself will be with them.

He will wipe every tear from their eyes, and there will be no more death or sorrow or crying or pain. All these things are gone forever."

And the one sitting on the throne said, "Look, I am making everything new!" And then he said to me, "Write this down, for what I tell you is trustworthy and true."

And he also said, "It is finished! I am the Alpha and the Omega—the Beginning and the End. To all who are thirsty I will give freely from the springs of the water of life.

All who are victorious will inherit all these blessings, and I will be their God, and they will be my children.
Revelation 21:3-7.

It is difficult for us to imagine what life will be like as Heaven and earth become joined.

We live in earthly bodies and we still see with corrupted vision but as we learn to put sin away from us and begin to clothe ourselves in Jesus, our eyes will also begin to see clearly and our understanding and experience will be refreshed.

Knowing what we now know about clothing ourselves with righteousness and overcoming the enemy, let us speedily develop a listening ear to what the Spirit is saying to us.

I will not attempt to install my own ideas of what this might look like in reality.

We can each allow the Spirit within us to widen our understanding of that picture and what it might involve for us.

Let us readily be guided into a life within God's kingdom and the New Jerusalem.

Where do our souls and spirits go when we die?

The question must inevitably be raised:

If we don't go to Heaven when we die, what happens to our bodies, spirits and our souls at that time?

We live in bodies that deteriorate.

If we die before Jesus returns, our bodies will return to the dust from where they came.

The Lord told the first man that he would return to the ground from where he came.

By the sweat of your brow will you have food to eat until you return to the ground from which you were made. For you were made from dust, and to dust you will return."
Genesis 3:19.

For those overcomers who are still alive when Jesus returns, our bodies will be changed to be like Jesus' new body.

Jesus was able to walk through walls, eat fish and break bread.

His new body retained the scars that He bore from giving His life for us.

He was able to show to Thomas the holes in His hands from the nails that had pierced Him and His side, through which a spear had been plunged.

Then he said to Thomas, "Put your finger here, and look at my hands. Put your hand into the wound in my side. Don't be faithless any longer. Believe!"
John 20:27.

He is also able to dwell with Father in a Heaven that is invisible to those outside.

We too may carry reminders of how we have served the Lord, where they are useful.

Our natural, unredeemed minds may find it difficult to comprehend such a way of living that defies natural laws.

Those overcomers who belong to Jesus, who are in the ground at that time, will be raised to be with us.

Their bodies too will be changed in the same way, to become Spiritual bodies.

Paul explained it to the Thessalonian Christians in this way:

Christ died for us so that, whether we are dead or alive when he returns, we can live with him forever.
1 Thessalonians 5:10.

And to the followers at Corinth:

But let me reveal to you a wonderful secret. We will not all die, but we will all be transformed!

It will happen in a moment, in the blink of an eye, when the last trumpet is blown. For when the trumpet sounds, those who have died will be raised to live forever. And we who are living will also be transformed.

For our dying bodies must be transformed into bodies that will never die; our mortal bodies must be transformed into immortal bodies.

Then, when our dying bodies have been transformed into bodies that will never die, this Scripture will be fulfilled: "Death is swallowed up in victory.
1 Corinthians 15:51-54.

When Jesus is revealed to the world, death will be swallowed up - there will be no more natural death for His children; the dead will be raised to eternity.

We have a difficulty when we read that word, eternity, because we have historically been taught that eternity means Heaven when we die, which in turn conjures up a variety of ideas that we associate with Heaven, somewhere else.

We often fail to grasp that Heaven is where God lives - it is His domain, and that God lives amongst a redeemed, righteous body of people, who are His temple.

When we read of Jesus' return from out of the clouds, we tend to imagine the natural clouds that are in our sky, but scripture describes clouds as being the abode of God - Heaven.

When Jesus returns from Heaven, Heaven is among the redeemed of God.

When Jesus returns, or is revealed, the righteous dead will be raised into that redeemed body of people where Heaven exists.

Jesus prayed: 'I pray Father that they will be one, as we are one'.

I pray that they will all be one, just as you and I are one - as you are in me, Father, and I am in you.

And may they be in us so that the world will believe you sent me.
John 17:21.

We fail to grasp that reality because it is not a revelation that we are generally taught, let alone live in the reality of.

We need to ask Father to redeem our minds like never before.

We are three parts: body, soul and spirit.

Our bodies will deteriorate and return to the dust; they are simply there for the temporary transportation of our soul and spirit.

Our soul is the essence that makes us; our mind, will and emotion.

If we allow God's Spirit to bring about the changes that are necessary in our lives, then our mind, will and emotion will also become redeemed; we will die to our flesh.

The second death will not harm us.

If we are stubborn and do not allow God's Spirit to bring about change then we will be harmed by the second death, as we have seen.

If we are born again of God's Spirit, we are, and will become, one with God and our Spirit becomes one with Father and Jesus.

We are wrapped up with Him.

If we die before Jesus is revealed in us; before we have allowed any change, our spirit and soul will be raised and will live forever with Him.

Our place in eternity will reflect the change that we have allowed the Spirit to bring about; how we have overcome the enemy who attempts to separate us from Jesus.

If we have used what we have been given wisely, we will be rewarded accordingly.

Jesus related a parable to describe this:

"Again, the Kingdom of Heaven can be illustrated by the story of a man going on a long trip.
He called together his servants and entrusted his money to them while he was gone.
He gave five bags of silver to one, two bags of silver to another, and one bag of silver to the last—dividing it in proportion to their abilities.
He then left on his trip.

"The servant who received the five bags of silver began to invest the money and earned five more.
The servant with two bags of silver also went to work and earned two more.

But the servant who received the one bag of silver dug a hole in the ground and hid the master's money.

"After a long time their master returned from his trip and called them to give an account of how they had used his money.

The servant to whom he had entrusted the five bags of silver came forward with five more and said, 'Master, you gave me five bags of silver to invest, and I have earned five more.'

"The master was full of praise.
'Well done, my good and faithful servant. You have been faithful in handling this small amount, so now I will give you many more responsibilities.
Let's celebrate together!'

"The servant who had received the two bags of silver came forward and said, 'Master, you gave me two bags of silver to invest, and I have earned two more.'

"The master said, 'Well done, my good and faithful servant.
You have been faithful in handling this small amount, so now I will give you many more responsibilities.
Let's celebrate together!'

"Then the servant with the one bag of silver came and said, 'Master, I knew you were a harsh man, harvesting crops you didn't plant and gathering crops you didn't cultivate.

I was afraid I would lose your money, so I hid it in the earth.
Look, here is your money back.'

"But the master replied, 'You wicked and lazy servant! If you knew I harvested crops I didn't plant and gathered crops I didn't cultivate, why didn't you deposit my money in the bank?

At least I could have gotten some interest on it.'
"Then he ordered, 'Take the money from this servant, and give it to the one with the ten bags of silver.

To those who use well what they are given, even more will be given, and they will have an abundance.

But from those who do nothing, even what little they have will be taken away.

Now throw this useless servant into outer darkness, where there will be weeping and gnashing of teeth.'
Matthew 25:14-30.

If we have buried our talent and have nothing of any worth to show for our lives, we may find that the little that we had will be removed from us.

When we overcome the enemy completely, Jesus will be revealed in us.

If we do not reveal Jesus in our lives now, we need to take stock and discover where God's Spirit wants to bring about change.

Our soul is either redeemed or it is not redeemed.

If we are redeemed then we will welcome God's Spirit, bringing about changes in those parts of our unredeemed mind, emotion and will, where the enemy still has control.

If we are not redeemed our soul and spirit will be raised at the last day for a different judgement.

Whilst we live, we eagerly await the coming of Jesus and make the most of the time that is passing.

But if our bodies die, time ceases to exist for us, and we live in eternity.

God lives in eternity as well, but chooses to step into our limited time dimension.

Our responsibility.

There will come a time when God will make judgments with regards to what we have done with the lives that we have been given.

We have talked about a false gospel that is not the good news that Jesus taught.

James had a word for those who chose to teach others:

Dear brothers and sisters, not many of you should become teachers in the church, for we who teach will be judged more strictly.
James 3:1.

Those who teach will be judged more strictly and so it would be wise to obtain good, true teaching in order to pass on to others what we know to be true.

Teachers have a greater responsibility and will be judged accordingly, but we all have a responsibility to weigh up what we are being taught.

We will not be let off with the excuse that we didn't know any different or that we had bad teachers.

Jesus said,' *I don't know you, 'depart from me you who practice iniquity'.*

If we are not listening to God's Spirit, we are not hearing and Jesus will disown us too.

Paul spoke about those who preach another gospel.

Let God's curse fall on anyone, including us or even an angel from Heaven, who preaches a different kind of Good News than the one we preached to you.

I say again what we have said before: If anyone preaches any other Good News than the one you welcomed, let that person be cursed.
Galatians 1:8-9.

Paul used strong language because he realised that God's plan of redemption would be undermined if it were allowed to continue.

God's plan has, in truth, been undermined, for centuries.

We are entering the age of God's kingdom.

If we want to be a part of building that kingdom then we will need to listen and to hear clearly what the Spirit is saying to those who would follow Him.

"So don't be afraid, little flock. For it gives your Father great happiness to give you the kingdom.
Luke 12:32.

We can move into His kingdom, or we can stay outside.

The Lord will never force us to make a move against our will.

He is calling us in love at this time, knocking on the door, asking to be allowed in.

When we open the door He will certainly come and dwell with us.

It is our choice.

Will we be the generation who welcome Jesus in?

Will we be the generation through whom the world will see Jesus?

The decision is ours to make.

Living in the new kingdom - God's kingdom - today.

How can we experience living in God's kingdom - eternity, today?

Many of us claim that we have crossed over into God's kingdom, but we live as if we have not.

This is often because we do not have an understanding of two things.
1. Where we have come from
2. Where we have come to.

This can be because the birth into our new life is not completed - we attempt to live with one leg in the enemy's kingdom and one leg in God's.

Perhaps we do not appreciate what occurred when we were baptised, or worse, we have not fully understood the condition we were in when we decided to follow Jesus and have not therefore appreciated our need of a saviour.

Many of us have not entered into the waters of baptism and have therefore not been born of water and Spirit.

Often teaching in this regard is scarce or flimsy.

There is much that we need to know in order to understand the spiritual aspect - what occurs in the spiritual realm when we are baptised by faith into Jesus.

Sadly many teachers do not have an understanding of the new life that Jesus offers or how to enter His kingdom and they pass their lack of knowledge and experience on.

There may be many other reasons for our inability to walk in God's kingdom.

If our foundations are not set on firm rock we are still sinking in confusion and ignorance.

In which case our victory over the enemy has failed and can not ever succeed until we begin to come to an understanding of who we are now, in Jesus.

We need revelation and we need to take action that will plant ourselves firmly within God's kingdom.

With regards to both I would recommend reading my book, Our Foundations, in order to make a start on the journey that we desire to set out on.

Until we have a rock to stand on - until we are fully aware of who we are, we will not be able to walk into God's kingdom, let alone live in the good of all that Jesus has done for us.

Do we live in the kingdom that Jesus taught? or are we living in deception - going through the routine of prayer and religious life, but in truth still living in the kingdom of death?

Are we living in victory - triumphant over the enemy?

What does our life look like?

Characteristics of living in the enemies kingdom

Depressions.
Psychological disorders.
Irrational fears.
Irrational behaviours.
Sleeping disorders.
Continual, repetitive illnesses.
Unhealthy dependencies.
Financial difficulties.
A lack of provision.
Breakdown of relationships.
Lifestyle addictions.
Lack of purpose.
Inability to succeed.
Fear of the unknown.
Inability to complete.
Unhealthy habits.
Lack of trust.
Insecurities.
Inability to make a judgement.
Double mindedness.
Eating disorders.

A need to control our environment and /or others around us.

An inability to control emotions.

Impatience, bad temper, sulking, jealousies, sexual deviances, lying, stealing, gossipping, speaking to the dead, perpetual grief, self harm, abusive relationships, unhappiness, aggressive behaviour, delving into psychic experiences, selfishness, etc.

We can add to the list of enemy activities in our lives but our aim is not to dwell on that kingdom of death but to appreciate that we have now been freed to come out of it.

If we have truly entered God's kingdom these are not our experience.

If they are, we need to address that.

We are born into God's kingdom in order to overcome the enemy, not to allow those fruits of sin and death to overcome us.

Characteristics of kingdom living:

Paul wrote about the fruits - the products of a life that is lived in God's Spirit:

Let me be clear, the Anointed One has set us free—not partially, but completely and wonderfully free!

We must always cherish this truth and stubbornly refuse to go back into the bondage of our past.

But the fruit produced by the Holy Spirit within you is divine love in all its varied expressions:
joy that overflows,
peace that subdues,
patience that endures,
kindness in action,
a life full of virtue,
faith that prevails,
gentleness of heart,
and strength of spirit.
Galatians 5:1,22⊦23 TPT

Paul also explained in his letters to the Corinthian Christians how love will be an increasing characteristic of our lives.

Do we love?

We are unable to with our own efforts, but God is love and so if we are living within His kingdom as one with Him, His love will also be a characteristic that will grow in us and will become abundantly clear in our own lives.

Love is patient and kind.
Love is not jealous or boastful or proud
or rude.
It does not demand its own way.

It is not irritable, and it keeps no record of being wronged.

It does not rejoice about injustice but rejoices whenever the truth wins out.

Love never gives up, never loses faith, is always hopeful, and endures through every circumstance.
1 Corinthians 13:4-7

Do we experience being able to love in this way particularly when we are being tested?

Do we respond to the promptings of His Spirit with us?

If we do not respond we are still living in the enemy's domain - we are living in rebellion.

We cannot live in two kingdoms.

Practicalities of daily life:

Every day presents a range of challenges and hurdles for us to either overcome or to be overwhelmed by.

The Lord is aware of all of these things and in truth has allowed them into our lives for a reason.

Are we overcomers, or are we defeated by those hurdles?

We have a choice.

The Lord will not allow anything into our life that we cannot, with Him, overcome.

But we often allow the lies of the enemy to persuade us that we are unable to overcome - we believe that our circumstances - the situations that we find ourselves in, are unchangeable.

Instead we must learn to trust in the one who can save us.

If we don't trust Him then perhaps we have not been born again - it is our faith in His saving power that has brought us into His kingdom.

Do we truly trust Him?

Do we need to rethink the basis of our faith?

A superficial pie in the sky faith will not produce life.

Having faith in a theology or an idea, in a doctrine or a religious group, will not bring us into a relationship with Jesus.

It is often for this very reason that we face challenges to our faith.

The Lord does not want us to live in unreality.

If the world is to see the manifestation of God's kingdom on the earth then we need to learn to live in faith.

It is faith that produces life that in turn will build kingdom - faith is creative.

When we lose our job, do we trust that God is our provider?

When we begin to learn to live in faith we can take the bread and fishes that seem to be such a small gift, in order to feed hundreds.

But we need to go through those times of trial and difficulty in order to become mature in our faith.

If we are not victorious in those things we will not move on into maturity - we may lose the prize that is waiting for us.

We have talked previously about many of the difficulties that are preventing God's kingdom from becoming visible to the world.

One of those difficulties is a lack of unity - there are many denominations and cliques.

It is within our ability to break those divisive issues and to pull down the man made structures that support them by our own actions - in the way we fellowship - socially interact, with each other - in the way we minister to each other outside of denominational barriers - outside of religious structures.

In short - in the way we bring love to each other.

We find at present that man is the centre of our spiritual activity - despite the external trappings that claim Jesus as being the focus, in truth, man clings on to control and organisation.

Jesus said, 'where two or three are together - there I am'!

For where two or three gather together as my followers, I am there among them."
Matthew 18:20.

If this is true for us then what need do we have of laity, clergy, pastors and leadership teams?

Man does not need to organise - to control, where Jesus is truly at the centre.

We need to learn to develop our individual ears, to hear what the Spirit is saying to each of us and to be released into our individual giftings.

This will only be possible as we gather in order to hear Him, and to respond to His personal leading.

We are used to being led by man - to sit, or stand, and wait, until we are bidden by man.

This is a form of religion that we must break free from.

"Don't let anyone call you 'Rabbi,' for you have only one teacher, and all of you are equal as brothers and sisters. Matthew 23:8

We will not become mature children of God by sitting in pews or by being spoon fed - our faith, our maturity will only come by flexing our own muscles.

What does God's kingdom look like?

Jesus taught about the kingdom all the time. We have many illustrations to describe what it looks like.

Our difficulty in envisioning it is often brought about by the confusion that has developed by our imagining that God's kingdom is Heaven.

In truth, God's kingdom has to do with earth as well as Heaven.

They are separate realms at present but when Jesus appears amongst us they will become one.

Jesus taught us how to establish God's kingdom - God's government, on earth.

When we live in righteousness, which isn't a sanctimonious idea - it is the reality of what we have been brought into.

Righteousness is simply living rightly.

It is living healthily - outside of the realm of the enemy - inside the realm of God.

Righteousness is living a life in faith, by responding to God's Spirit.

Jesus sent God's Spirit in order to enable us to live in this way. It is not an impossible task but it is reality.

There are some today who are moving towards God's kingdom.

There are some who delight in the King.

There are some who are hearing Him.

There are some who are learning to respond when He speaks.

Will we?

When we do, the prayer that Jesus asked us to pray will soon be answered.

'Your kingdom come, Your will be done, on earth as it is in Heaven'.

May your Kingdom come soon. May your will be done on earth, as it is in heaven.
Matthew 6:10.

I will leave you with some words from another author in giving an explanation of the letter written to the Hebrew Christians in exile.

Hebrews 8: 1-6.

Jesus is seated in honour beside the throne of the majestic God where He ministers in the Heavenly Tabernacle, which is the true place of worship.

If the Heavenly Tabernacle is the true place of worship, it is where we need to find ourselves. The human priests offer sacrifices in an earthly tabernacle. But Jesus offers true worship in the Heavenly one.

Human priests belong to the old covenant of Moses which no longer has any power to bring us to God. It is only Jesus who can bring us into the presence of God.

Today, everyone is welcome to enter into the Holy of Holies and to come before the throne of grace.

God wants us to enter in and meet with Him. But many do not experience this place of true worship.

What prohibits us is that this is not a place we can see with our physical eyes. It is a spiritual domain. And we do not know how to enter into the spiritual realm.

Jesus teaches us that the kingdom of God is within us.

It is not the physical world we see or "eating and drinking" (Romans 14:17).

It is not the meetings we attend where we sing songs and listen to preachers. As enjoyable as they are, they do not usually take us into the presence of God.

In fact, those meetings are a shadow of what God really wants us to enjoy.

The kingdom of God is revealed by our godly character of love, joy and peace. But the spiritual dimension of the kingdom of God is where we find the gifts of the Holy Spirit such as healing, miracles, prophecy and the ability to travel through time and space in the way Philip did when he ministered to the Ethiopian eunuch (Acts 8:39).

It is this realm of the Spirit of God which is so elusive to many.
We might have an experience of being baptised in Him one day and have a revelation of the love and presence of God.

But if we do not continue to be filled with the Holy Spirit, we will not retain that experience for long.

The first time we are baptised in the Holy Spirit is not the finished product. It is only a door which opens the opportunity of a life-long experience of living in His presence.

The presence of God is available as we continue to live in Him.

It is only when we individually seek His presence that we find Him.

It is possible to seek God when there are many others with us.

But if we depend on someone else to provide music and songs in order to find God, it is probable that all we will experience is an enjoyable emotional high.

The point is that Jesus has opened the door for us.

He has sat down at the right hand of God as a continuous mediator for us.

When we come to Him in faith, He ushers us into the presence of God where we can enjoy fellowship.

(Taken from The Book of Hebrews by J.J. Sweetman).

There are always further questions and enquiries to be made in the Christian life – everything is new!

There is always something to discover – something new to share with others.

Please feel free to email me if you have any questions, or would like to talk about this book.

To contact Tim - the author:
email: warwickhouse@mail.com

Tim has also written:

Journey Into Life:

What did Jesus really preach about when He was on earth?
Within "A Journey into Life" we discover the joy of travelling to a new place.

Tim has set our search for God's kingdom in the form of a journey to a new land.

Once inside the new land we begin a journey of discovery – everything is new.

Did Jesus teach that His kingdom is within our grasp?
Is this a land – A kingdom that we can live in now – in our own lifetime?

The answer is yes!

Some Adjustments Required?:

We live our lives from day to day carrying out regular routines and rituals often without thinking about what we do and what we say and why.

We take for granted that the things that we have done and said and even for centuries past must be correct because that is simply the way things are.

Tim has taken some of the many misunderstood concepts in the Christian life that we have, for so long, taken for granted and brought correction and redirection.

God is doing a new thing in this season and those who want to follow His direction need to hear Him.

A Time To Consider:

A Time to consider was written at a time when several friends and friends of friends had been taken Ill by potentially life threatening illnesses.

When this happens to us out of the blue it is naturally a shocking discovery to realise that we aren't going to live on this earth, in this body, forever.

It is however a reality that we all need to take into consideration.

Any of us may be taken away at any time.
Our life on earth is a very short period when we consider eternity.

Let us get involved with eternity now - we may not get another opportunity to do so.

The Shaking:

We live in a changing era.
God is moving and the earth is being shaken.
The church age is passing.
God's kingdom age is upon us.
How do the times that we live fit with God's plan for us in eternity?
Has our own past affected our present and will it affect our future?
Can we make an impact in our time?

Our Foundations:

Many of us have missed out on vital foundational truths in our walk with the Lord.
Consequently we tend to wander around unaware that we may be missing out on the good things that Father has planned for us, unsure of where we should be or what our purpose is here on earth.
As we look into "Our Foundations" some much needed clarity and understanding will be gleaned for our benefit and for that of the emerging kingdom.

Genesis part one:

There are many apparent mysteries for us to uncover when reading the book of Genesis.

In Genesis part one we attempt to uncover and give an answer to some of these mysteries.

We also invite the reader to consider the text for themselves and to appreciate that the Lord is wanting us to open up a discussion with Him.

Genesis part two:

In Genesis part two we continue to look at the line of progression that began with Adam and will continue to the birth of Jesus.

Noah has journeyed into a new era. Life has continued as the Lord promised.

Abraham, the man of faith and the father of all who choose to trust in Jesus, is born.

The nations begin to emerge from the mists.

Genesis part three:

Genesis part three brings us to the birth of Isaac who is a type of Jesus.

From Isaac, through Jacob, to Joseph and into the land of Egypt we can journey with the patriarchs and the children of the man who becomes Israel.

The Lord is bringing His plan of redemption to pass.

The End Times - for non Christians.

The end times for non Christians spells out, in a relatively short book, the times that we are living in now and the part that non Christians have to play at the end of this age.

Entering Eternity Today.

Do we go to Heaven when we die?

For over two thousand years there has been some considerable misunderstanding and confusion with regards to God's kingdom.

Where it is taught, the question is inevitably raised, what is God's kingdom?
Is it a place we go to when we die?

Will we be taken there one day?
The answer to that one is a definite, no.

The enemy has introduced much incorrect teaching into church circles in order to ensure that his kingdom remains.

When we uncover the truth of this deception and learn to live in God's promises he will flee like never before and the world will encounter a harvest unlike any other.

The Thief.

As Christians, our basic beliefs and understandings are grounded in the interpretation of the scriptures that are made by a few well meaning theologians.

But what happens to those basic foundations of truth when we discover that perhaps not all of those translations have been well made?

How great a part has the enemy of our faith played in the interpretation and representation of the scriptures that we read everyday in our Bibles?

We may find that we are living at a time when our understanding of scripture requires some adjustment if we are to enter into all that Father has in store for us.

Other recommended publications of related interest:

By John J Sweetman

Paperback and EBooks:

Establishing the kingdom series:

The Book of Joshua
The Book of Judges
The Book of Ruth
The Book of 1 Samuel
The Book of 2 Samuel
The Book of 1 Corinthians
The Book of 2 Corinthians
The Book of Galatians
The Book of Revelations
The Book of Romans
The Book of Hebrews
The Emerging kingdom

Babylon or Jerusalem – your choice

by Fiona Sweetman

Paperback and EBook
Taste the Colour Smell the Number

Printed in Great Britain
by Amazon

81554076R00119